Perfect Hire Blueprint by Dave C

Edited by Julie Chakrin

Published by mPower Advisors

61 Pleasant Street #1453

Newburyport MA 01950

www.PerfectHireBlueprint.com

© 2017 Dave Clough

TRUDY, WE MAKE A GREAT TEAM. I THINK WE ACCOMPLISHED A LOT. GOOD LUCK WITH ALL YOUR FUTURE ENDEAVORS!

Contents

Thank you for picking up this book! Feel free to read it from front to back, or jump to a chapter as a reference for your hiring needs at any time. For more information, and to download the resources mentioned in the book, visit PerfectHireBlueprint.com/Resources.

To your success,

Dave

Foreword

There are a few "Meta skills" that make a person's life and business SIGNIFICANTLY better.

The ability to really know what drives and motivates or frustrates and challenges another human being is at the top of the list...especially for Entrepreneurs!

I have spent 30 years serving over 40,000 people to discover exactly that for themselves and apply it to their life and business.

It is one thing to help individuals discover these truths about themselves. It is an entirely different thing to systematically and objectively discover what truly drives and challenges another human being, and strategically match their gifts to a career where they can shine...for the organization they work for and themselves.

Amazing!

The book you are holding will do exactly that.

I have had the privilege of working with and supporting Dave and I am always impressed with how he thinks, his ability to make the overwhelming and difficult seem simple, how he solves problems and how he cares about people...their abilities and their needs.

The Perfect Hire Blueprint presents a powerful step by step process that when applied properly saves entrepreneurs and businesses time, frustration and significant money. The value of this process is easy to underestimate. I want to remind you that if you are holding this book, you are likely in the middle of hiring – and perhaps building an entire team. The truth is, you will do it right or you will pay dearly.

A study conducted by the Center for American Progress determined that the cost of losing an employee can range anywhere from 16% of their salary (for hourly, unsalaried employees), to 213% of the salary (for a highly trained position)! ***So if a highly trained executive is making $120,000 a year, the true loss could be up to $255,600 to the company!***

The reality is this: small to medium size businesses cannot afford to makes these kind of mistakes.

I know this for a fact, since I have been hiring and building teams for over 30 years. I can say with great certainty (personal experience) that in the past I have made almost every mistake this book aims to solve.

Following just some of Dave's systems (like integrating the DISC Assessment as part of the hiring process) has helped me hire team members that are still with me over 20 years later.

One last recommendation: please do yourself and your business a favor, don't just read the book – engage with the online resources. The tools are all there to actually do this, to find the right person for the right job...the first time! Like I just did with my new Executive Assistant.

I will leave you with one of my favorite quotes of Dave's:

"Most companies hire based on experience and skill, but they fire based on attitude or behavior."

Let's not make that mistake again.

Enjoy!

Jay Fiset

Facilitator, Mastermind Mentor & Best Selling Author

www.MastermindtoMillions.com

Prologue

Writing a book is not something that most people do on a whim, so you may be wondering why someone with my background decided to write this.

Simon Sinek recently wrote the book *Start with Why* – I totally buy in to his concepts, so I'll start this book with my "why."

My why, and my passion, is to help small businesses (1 to 350 employees) succeed. That is my full time job. I left corporate America to do just that - to become a business advisor (some people might use the words consultant or coach).

The reason I care so much about small businesses is because they are an economic equalizer and a way to change your station in life. Robert Kiyosaki's book *Rich Dad, Poor Dad* emphasizes that just a paycheck will not change your station in life, but owning a business very well could.

I came from a modest background (my family was on food stamps and free school lunches) and dramatically improved my station, but I did it the way most people would expect:

Dave's path

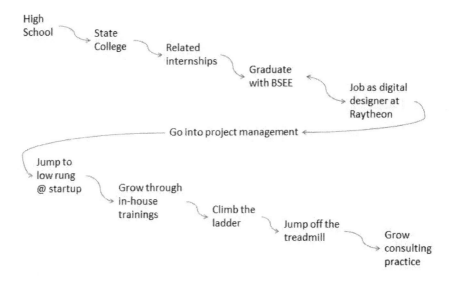

It was a bit of a fluke for me to be on this path, hailing from a blue collar town with blue collar parents. Just attending college was unexpected, given the underprivileged high school in my town.

Many of the small business CEOs/owners that I've worked with have not gone the college route, and I think my upbringing allows me to connect with them.

My stepfather bought a small business when I was young, but it wasn't a viable business for very long. All of these factors have played a part in forming my "why."

The odds are not in the favor of the small business. We've all heard the data: 20%+ of small businesses fail after one year and less than 1/3 make it to 10 years.

Those are terrible odds, yet people start businesses all the time. Back in 2004 I did it too, so I guess I'm one of the successful third.

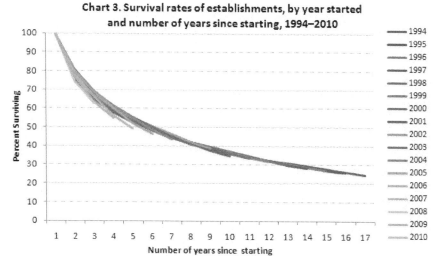

Chart 3. Survival rates of establishments, by year started and number of years since starting, 1994–2010

Source: U.S. Bureau of Labor Statistics

The typical reason for failure isn't because the idea was bad. It is usually because the execution was poor. I work hard to get entrepreneurs to focus on the right things at the right times.

This brings me to hiring: bad hiring plays a huge part in the execution issues that cause small businesses to fail. It's important to hire the right people who fit the job AND the company.

There is a saying I like: "don't hire for skill, hire for attitude." The skills can be learned by those with some aptitude. While this is generally true, for a small business owner, this is too simplistic because they don't have the time or the resources to train every employee.

Small businesses need the attitude AND the skill, but most small businesses don't know how to find the right people. The whole reason they may fail is because they hired the wrong people (and likely had a poor business plan).

If a business is going to succeed, it needs the right people doing the right jobs, and that is why I'm writing this book.

I've been able to achieve a life that I did not foresee as a child, and my hope is that this book helps at least a few more entrepreneurs achieve their visions and goals.

Introduction

Has this ever happened to you?

You need to hire someone now because your employees are busy, stressed, and you'll lose money and your best workers if you don't get more help. So you ask around, and someone you know suggests a candidate who they think will be a perfect fit. Maybe this person is a friend or a relative, and you get the feeling that he might not be exactly right, but you need someone to fill the role immediately or your business will suffer. To make it more official, you ask a manager to "interview" the person to get a feel for talent and fit, but there are no solid criteria.

Nobody at your company has the time to train, so you do on the job training. You hope the employee will succeed, but after 90 days it is clear that he is the wrong fit. You don't want to fire the person since it will cause hurt feelings and a strained personal relationship, so you keep trying to make it work.

When you ultimately have to fire the person, now you've lost 3+ months, not to mention the financial losses of finding someone new to hire and train. The cost of this bad hire is in the tens of thousands of dollars in direct cost and opportunity costs.

The U.S. Department of Labor estimated that the average cost of a bad hiring decision can equal 30% of the individual's first year potential earnings, and that is the lowest number that I've seen. In 2013, CareerBuilder surveyed 6000 hiring managers and HR professionals worldwide. They found that 27% of employers in the U.S. who had a bad hire reported costs exceeding $50,000.

* * *

The cost of a bad hire can be in the tens of thousands in direct cost and opportunity costs.

* * *

Go to <u>PerfectHireBlueprint.com/Resources</u> for a spreadsheet to help calculate the cost of a bad hire for your business.

It doesn't have to be this way.

In a growing company, hiring seems to be a never ending process, taking up a lot of time. In my experience, most hiring managers dislike the process of hiring. For these people, it feels like running uphill: painful while doing it, but rewarding when the process is complete and after some recovery time.

I've spoken with many who feel that even after all the hard work (much of it after hours) and due diligence, it is still a gamble as to whether the person is a good hire. After the long process, some employers feel that they still need to put the person on a 90 day trial and withhold benefits until the employee has proven himself.

There is a major problem with the idea of a trial hire: the best candidates do not want to be on a trial with little clarity. Why would they leave a good job for a new one with an uncertain 90 day outcome? But if an employer does not do this trial, how can he protect the company from overpaying or getting locked into a bad hire?

Does this sound like you?

Without the right people in your company, everything is a struggle. How many of these sound like what you are experiencing?

- You have to micromanage to get the desired results
- You have to repeat yourself because they "don't remember"
- You can't take a vacation because things fall apart when you are gone
- When you are out of the office, the productivity drops
- If you are not looking over shoulders, nothing gets done
- To the employees, it's just a job
- Employees are always asking for a raise, but the productivity and profitability is not increasing
- You don't want to praise, because they'll want a raise
- You have to double check everything before it is sent to the customer (internal or external)
- A person does one part of the job well, but the rest is a mess
- The manager reporting to you can't get the results from the employees that you did before your promotion
- Employees just don't have the right attitude
- Sometimes it is a struggle to be motivated to go in to the office

With the right employees, things are much better:

- People are productive and profitable
- They seem to know what to do without you having to tell them
- It isn't just a job; they care about the company

- The customers are happy and they refer you to their contacts
- Your company is growing, and you don't feel as if you have to push too hard.
- It is easier to find people to hire because your employees speak well of the company
- Problems are solved before you are told about them
- Employees work together easily and push each other to do better
- Morale is good
- It is a pleasure to go to work

Of course, the second list also requires good management and leadership, but that is beyond the scope of this book. If you don't have the right people, you can still fail even though you are a great leader.

This book is written for leaders who need to hire and want to build a team that achieves great things.

It is for the leader who recognizes that it is better to get scalable results through people than getting self-recognition for personally doing the work. It is for those who are willing to invest in others for long-term success, rather than those who need quick results that require micromanagement.

When businesses grow, they need more people. But the speed at which a business grows and the ease with which it grows depends upon its ability to hire and retain high quality people. **I am NOT a commissioned recruiter.** I primarily consult with and advise small business owners to help them grow their businesses. In most cases they can't achieve the goals that we set without the right people in place. As Jim Collins (author of *Good to Great*) says, "We need to have the right people in the right seats."

I believe in continuous improvement, and I practice what I preach. What got me started was reading *The 7 Habits of Highly Effective People* by Steven Covey in the early 1990s. It was my awakening as a young manager. Since then I have filled bookshelves with business books. I continually refer to Covey, Collins, Ken Blanchard, Peter Drucker, Daniel Goleman and John Maxwell and have recently added Brendon Burchard. My views are a distillation of my learning, and I use these as well as the talents I was given and my experience to do my best to advise my clients.

Sometimes we need to hire senior level managers because those roles don't already exist in the company. Other times we need to hire beneath the person we want to act as a manager so that she can stop doing the work and start leading a team to do the work, giving an opportunity for personal and professional growth.

There have also been times I have diagnosed that the wrong person is in an important role. We need to either relocate or replace that person in order to achieve the company's goals. In all of these cases it is essential to hire the right person. My goal is to help my client find and hire the right person for the job without overpaying to do so.

In many cases, these clients could do the job of hiring internally – if only they knew how. For many companies, there's no need to use professional recruiters to find good people. A structured, thoughtful hiring process is necessary because most of my clients have either never hired well, or haven't hired frequently enough to do it well consistently.

There are many factors that can make hiring more difficult:

- It takes a lot of time that most managers believe they don't have
- It typically requires calls outside of normal work hours
- In order to engage with good candidates, you need to move fast
- Resumes are sometimes works of fiction, "edited" by experts
- The candidate interview is a coached performance rather than an authentic conversation, and you may not know the real person until many days after he starts
- References are either friends or past coworkers who won't (or can't) tell you the truth
- Recruiters and headhunters are compensated or incentivized to fill the position regardless of whether the person is the best fit
- The hiring manager goes with his gut, thinking he is a good judge of character.

Bad hires often occur because the hiring manager goes with his gut. Research shows that people are not as good at judging other people as they think they are. The person who hires by trusting his gut tends to ignore other information, so good hiring is inconsistent at best.

I've worked with many successful entrepreneurs who succeeded even when they had no education in running a business. Some have been tradesman, and others have been professionals like doctors and lawyers.

While they all have a different number of years of education, the one thing that makes them similar is the lack of formal business training. They all know their area of expertise very well, and that is a big part of their success. But they will typically say that they got to this point by going with their gut. They will also hire based on their gut.

When your brain recalls an experience from the past, positive or negative, you can get a gut feeling. It may just feel like butterflies, but for intense situations it can be more extreme. Some people may be very much in tune with the intensity of these feelings; others are not.

Science tells us that this "gut check" is all based upon past experience stored in the brain. The more experiences you've had (this tends to coincide with age), the more likely it is that you've "seen this before." We learn from our experiences.

There are a lot of moving parts in trying to "read" a candidate: manipulation, environmental factors, half-truths, and medication.

Some people can get away with trusting their gut, and others shouldn't. Emotional Intelligence (EI), the ability to understand and implement the feelings and emotions of yourself and others, can help in hiring. Some are naturally high in EI. For those who are not, it's possible to actively work to better understand the feelings and emotions of oneself and others.

So how can a company build a reliable hiring process around intuition or gut feeling? People who trust their gut tend to ignore data and facts. The gut overrides all other information. If we accept for a moment that the hiring manager can count on his gut, how does he integrate the information from the rest of the interview team? Making decisions on gut feeling is not only unreliable, it's also not scalable.

How does a new hiring manager develop the same level of gut feel that works for those with more experience, or make successful hires? For good hiring decisions, there needs to be more data, and

in the Perfect Hire Blueprint process, this data comes from
Assessments.

While the in-person interview is critical to hiring the best people,
it is only one piece of the puzzle. A research-based Assessment will
give much more insight into the candidate. A good unbiased
Multi-Measure Assessment, like the one I use (TriMetrix HD), will
allow companies to more fully understand if the candidate will be
a good fit for the company and the job.

The graphic below from the Harvard Business Review shows the
research behind this information. No one activity has a 100%
correlation to job performance, and that is why Multi-Measure
Assessments, reference checks, the resume, and the interview are
necessary.

THE MOST EFFECTIVE HIRING SELECTION PRACTICES
And those that don't work so well, based on validity coefficients ranging from 0 to 1. The higher the
number, the higher the correlation between test scores and predicted job performance.

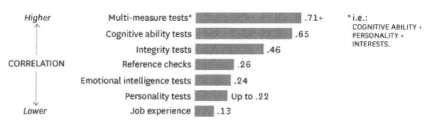

Higher	Multi-measure tests*	.71+
	Cognitive ability tests	.65
	Integrity tests	.46
CORRELATION	Reference checks	.26
	Emotional intelligence tests	.24
	Personality tests	Up to .22
Lower	Job experience	.13

* i.e.: COGNITIVE ABILITY + PERSONALITY + INTERESTS.

SOURCE BASED ON DATA SHARED BY FRANK L SCHMIDT IN A NOV 6, 2013 ADDRESS TO PTCMW
AS AN UPDATE TO: SCHMIDT, F. L. & HUNTER, J. E. (1998).   HBR.ORG

Can't I Just Hire a Headhunter?

Some think that headhunters, also known as contract recruiters, are the solution, but I don't believe that they are.

If you are as avid a sports fan as I am, you may be aware of Scott Boras. He's the guy who tends to get the highest priced contracts for star baseball players. These players tend to become mercenaries – moving to the team who will pay the highest price and considering little else.

If you were a team owner, would you want Scott Boras to represent your players? I don't think so – mercenaries are not loyal to their current employer once their contract ends.

My point is that headhunters (high commissioned recruiters) are a lot like Scott Boras: they are incentivized to get the highest salary possible when placing a candidate, and poach that person soon after to place her in another company. If the employee doesn't leave, she may ask for much more money. This leads to a mercenary mentality rather than one of a loyal, long-term employee.

As a leader, you can see why this is a poor method for growing a thriving business.

We recently hired an Engineer for a client using the Perfect Hire Blueprint. With a targeted Job Ad built from the Benchmark Assessment, we were able to narrow the field down to a few GREAT candidates and make a perfect hire in just a few weeks:

CASE STUDY

Client - R&D Tax Credits

We recently hired an Engineer for a client using the Perfect Hire Blueprint. With a targeted Job Ad built from the Benchmark Assessment, we were able to narrow the field down to a few GREAT candidates and make a perfect hire in just a few weeks.

41 Days from **JOB POST** TO **CLOSE**

<$90 TOTAL COST **TO PLACE JOB ADS**

16 GOOD APPLICANTS

5 Phone Screens

4 In-person Interviews

2 Finalists

1 Job Offer:

A-PLAYER ENGINEER

A successful hiring process such as the one I have outlined in this book can be executed by a company of any size to find A-players. Yes, finding the right person takes time, energy, passion and coordination, but the Return on Investment (ROI) is worth it. Your work team can go from good to great by getting the right players on the bus.

The Right People on the Bus in the Right Seats

What if every employee you hired was a perfect and productive fit for the job? Managing them would be easier and the group would be more productive, making the company more profitable. Wouldn't that be great? **The Perfect Hire Blueprint can help achieve that.**

I work with companies all the time that don't have the right person in the position. Maybe it isn't that they are incompetent or unproductive – it could just be that they are a wrong fit for this particular job. Maybe they are a Swiss Army Knife – they can do lots of different things, but are optimized for none of them.

Most jobs would be more productive with a specialist, and it is usually much easier to find and train someone for one job than finding many Jacks-of-all-trades who can perform at each job.

Of course, the more likely case is that you have an employee doing a job and it just isn't working as expected. It could be that you moved someone into the job to try to make it work, but in most cases the person was hired for the job and it is not working.

- How much time is spent trying to make that work?
- How much money is being spent on this position?

- What is the opportunity cost of not having someone who is qualified in the position – how much is being lost?

You may think that you are doing someone a favor by putting them in that position, but this isn't good for you, him, or the company in the long run. FIX IT NOW!

You agree that you need to hire the right person, but how can you do it? You have a track record of mixed results. **The Perfect Hire Blueprint process is the answer.** It has been proven by many consultants, recruiters and managers who have hired thousands of people. Why not use something that has a 90+% success rate vs. a typical hiring process that is about 50% successful?

There are some who have a good track record of hiring that don't use this kind of process, but even if you have one good hiring manager, the others usually do not see that level of success.

I was one of those successful hiring managers who hired across multiple groups in one company. I think that was my legacy – more than anything else I contributed to the company. Most of the people I hired for this high-tech company from 1994 until 2003 are still employed there. But with all of my success, I still made one big mistake. I had honed a process and my instincts over the years, but one candidate got through who ended up being a failure at the company, and I've never forgotten it.

I hired someone I knew socially and with whom I played basketball. He was a great point guard. He had great presence, good instincts, and a decent way about him. I was not objective – I was blind to signs that he was not a good fit. The job I hired him to do was in technical support. If you've ever worked in customer support, the ideal employee for this position and the ideal solution for the customer is FAST.

Unfortunately, this candidate valued high quality over speed, and his level of quality took way too much time. He could handle less than half the volume that others did. Within 6 months of his employment, it was clear that this had to change. We had a discussion at this point, and continued to have these discussions at least monthly. Before the first year, he had found another job, which was the best outcome I could have anticipated. I never calculated the full cost of this bad hire, but needless to say, I never took a shortcut in hiring again.

My primary point is that we all are biased. Our past continues to shape our future. One bad encounter may cause us to shy away from anything that reminds us of the encounter. Conversely, a good outcome can bias us to try to repeat what worked, but each is just a data point; not a trend. Continuously good results are a trend, and an objective process delivers on that.

Science-based Assessments have been proven to be unbiased and to improve any hiring process. In addition to the biases mentioned above, the Assessments cannot put any class of people at an advantage or disadvantage. The Assessments that I use have been proven to have no bias toward gender, race, age, disability or those with military service (see the TTI adverse impact study at PerfectHireBlueprint.com/Resources).

Assessments must comply with The Equal Employment Opportunity Commission (EEOC) guidelines and those of the Office of Federal Contract Compliance Programs (OFCCP) if the company has government contracts.

Hiring decisions that are made based on information from the candidate's interview, experience, background, references, behavior, values, skill set and acumen are the most informed. If you remove any of these, the risk of a bad hire is greatly increased.

How the Process Evolved

Over the past 25 years I've hired some fantastic people. The process I started using was that of the company for which I worked, and I have evolved this process over the years. I have made a couple of mistakes in hiring, but I have not made the same mistakes twice. To a great extent, the people I've hired have performed well, and many are still in the same companies and roles today. That kind of retention is a testament to getting the right people in the right seats.

With that said, I was never satisfied with the process. Looking back, I seemed to have a knack for recognizing the right people, but it was hard to teach that instinct to other managers. I've always wanted a system that was repeatable so that the wrong people did not get into the companies for which I worked. This system has continued to evolve as I've added key pieces along the way (including Benchmarking and great Assessments), and has come together to produce the Perfect Hire Blueprint.

Hiring great people is the lifeblood of a growing company. Employing more people leads to more leverage, which results in higher profit down the road. The better the person fits in the role, the more profitable the company will be, and a company can't grow if it can't find good people.

If the leadership has found a desired niche, the demand for the product or service will warrant more people to build and deliver it. For fortunate companies, the demand requires that they hire because they have outgrown the capabilities of the current staff, and the increased cash flow makes for an easy decision to hire more people.

Hiring the right people for the right positions will allow your company to grow. If you hire the wrong people, you could lose the momentum that got you here – and you'll need that momentum to reach your next business goal. There is a lot at stake. Doesn't it make sense to increase the odds of success with a repeatable process that works?

Let's dive into the Perfect Hire Blueprint!

Chapter 1: Preparing to Hire

You've determined that you want to hire someone. Now let's double check that it makes sense. This decision should not be taken lightly, yet many companies that I work with can't reach their goals unless they get more of the right people.

Questions to Ask Before Hiring

There are so many things to worry about:

- Is now the right time to hire another person?
- Is there a long-term need for the position?
- Is part-time the right answer?
- Can we afford another person on the payroll?
- Is the needed skill set available?
- Where do I look to find the right person?
- What if the talent we need is too expensive?
- Can I offer a competitive package?
- Will our culture change with new people and growth?
- Can we properly onboard and train this person when we are all so busy?
- How much will it cost to find this person (job posting sites, headhunters, recruiters, temp agencies, paying people to look at hundreds of resumes, paying people to interview candidates, ramp-up time)?
- What interview questions can be asked and what can't be asked legally?
- How will those who interact with the new employee feel about sharing information and recognition?

- What if we train someone and he leaves for the competition?
- What are the consequences if we don't hire anyone?

...no wonder companies procrastinate and don't look forward to hiring!

What Are the Costs of Hiring?

The cost of hiring is more than just the total compensation of the person you hire. There is a real, tangible cost to hiring. Many managers procrastinate on hiring because they and their team are already too busy, and the thought of adding an additional top priority to the already full plate is daunting.

In addition to the focus that hiring the right person takes, the cost of the hiring process is not insignificant. Here is a list of tangible costs to recruit and hire a candidate (opportunity costs are additional):

1. Developing the ad (time/salaries for all involved in drafting the ad)
2. Headhunter/recruiter fees (hourly if on-site, or up to 30+% of 1 year of salary if a headhunter – wide range of $5K to $100K, depending on the position.)
3. Placing the ad strategically (salary or outsource expense, and cost of postings online and offline – at least a few hundred dollars per month)
4. Tracking and filtering the candidates (tracking software, filtering time in data entry, wading through applicant info, and sending filtering email, scheduling calls, phone screening)

5. Paying your A-players to interview candidates (time/salaries for your top performers)
6. Paying your A-players for the roundtable discussion on candidates (time/salaries for your top performers)
7. Travel expenses for candidates (just mileage if local, but airfare, hotel, car, and meals if not)
8. Cost of getting the offer approved (typically more than one manager at a bigger company)
9. Relocation and sign-on bonus, if applicable (immediate expenses).

What happens if you find the right candidate, but she does not accept? You still have all the expenses above except for #1 and #2 if using a headhunter. Otherwise these expenses continue to add up.

Reactive Recruiting vs. Talent Acquisition

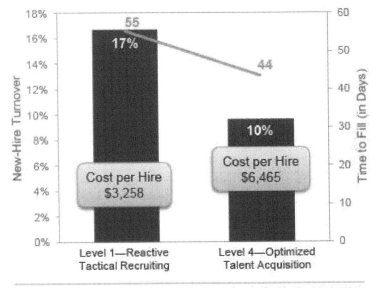

Source: *Bersin by Deloitte, 2014.*

In 2014, a study by Bersin by Deloitte found that organizations at the highest level of talent acquisition maturity spend two times more per hire in less time compared to those with the lowest effectiveness. But that is just the upfront cost. Their return on good hiring and onboarding processes far exceeds that of the reactive hiring companies.

What is the best way to keep your expenses down yet find the right A-player for your job opening? Fish for the right candidates where they can be found (see chapter 7 on Sourcing), and get the first great candidate to accept. The latter may require spending more than you originally budgeted, but it may be cheaper than looking for another candidate.

Of course, having a plan B (another A-player as a close second) is the best strategy if you can make that happen. Then it is a value decision: if primary candidate does not take a fair offer, hopefully your backup candidate will. Having two (or more) great candidates can help you stay in budget.

If you are looking for a purple unicorn (skills that are in short supply), it will cost even more. People who are this much in demand are not looking at job boards, so active recruiting is needed to find the passive talent (more on this in chapter 7: Sourcing).

To do hiring right, it must be a priority. **Speed is your friend when hiring**, so the hiring manager needs to be available when the candidates are available, and that is likely to include nights and weekends for telephone discussions, email exchanges and in-person meetings.

* * *

To do hiring right, it must be a priority. Speed is your friend when hiring.

* * *

Hiring the Right People

Hiring the right people is the one of the biggest business problems today. In an economic expansion cycle like the one we are currently experiencing as of this writing, businesses need more good people:

- Large businesses need more people for the company to earn more so they can report those earnings to their shareholders,
- VC funded startups need to hit milestones in order to get the next chunk of funding, and
- Small businesses need people to keep up with demand in a fast-growing company.

But most businesses struggle with hiring the right people. The typical hiring process rarely delivers consistent results of acquiring A-players.

It's easy for a candidate to "game the system" to present himself as someone he is not.

- The resume and cover letters may not have been created by the candidate, or may have been "massaged" by a friend, family member, or career coach with more experience in crafting these documents. They often stretch the truth, to put it mildly.

- The interview is just a performance – a well-coached interaction when the candidate is on her best behavior (and/or medication), which may not be consistent if hired.
- The typical reference checking calls are useless because the reference is not objective and knows not to say anything negative. Or you might just be directed to HR.

If a candidate spends just a few minutes searching Google for interview strategies, here are some typical articles she'd find:

- Interviewing Tips: How To Maximize Your Effectiveness
- Substitution: An Interview Performance Technique Borrowed From Acting
- The Science of Nailing the Interview
- How to Answer The 25 Most Important Interview Questions
- How To Take Control Of The Interview
- What NOT to Say in an Interview
- 5 Ways to Sell Yourself While Answering "Do You Have Any Other Questions?"
- The Perfect Resume: Quantify & Qualify

And that's all from just one free site.

With all this guidance of what to say and what not to say, how do you get to know the real person? One article talks specifically about acting! Given that many interviewers have made up their mind **within 90 seconds**, all a candidate has to do is manage or "take control of" the first few minutes, and he's in.

The hiring manager must change the game to get additional insight into the candidate.

The good news is that we have developed a process that delivers a 90%+ chance of hiring success.

A significant key to hiring success is the Assessment portion of the process. *I've personally hired more than 75 people and have assessed and/or helped select maybe a thousand more.* This process is the culmination of what worked, lessons learned from what didn't work, and information from other hiring resources with proven results.

Defining "Mis-fits"

So far I've referred to good hires and bad hires, but let's be clear. A bad hire is not necessarily a bad person. You should give yourself and your team more credit than to say you hired a bad person. That person was just not right for your company or the position. The person may be fine in another culture and job.

Benchmark
(a profile of the
right person)

Mis-fit™

Perfect Hire

Going forward, I'm going to refer to a bad hire as a Mis-fit™. This bad hire was a bad fit, a mistake, hence a Mis-fit™.

On the opposite end of the hiring scale is a great hire, and we should make that clear as well.

You Want A-players

Perhaps you've heard the saying, "**A-players attract other A-players. B-players attract C-players**." What does that mean? First, my definitions:

A-players are driven to succeed. They are typically goal oriented. They consistently get the job done on time without a manager looking over their shoulder. They may have some setbacks, but they learn from them.

A-players challenge each other. There may be informal, friendly competitions, and while that can cause minor problems, wanting to better a coworker raises one's competency.

A-players seek continuous improvement, and they put in the work knowing that the payoff will be in the long term. That payoff is personal for them; it might be monetary, experience for a desired position, or freedom from oversight to name a few common goals.

A-players are typically smart, but that doesn't necessarily equate to their GPAs from college. Book smart doesn't always ensure that the person will be job smart (some use the term street smart, but I won't, as not to confuse with those who can survive on their own in a city).

I have worked with many high IQ people who have not performed at the level of others with lower GPAs from schools of a lower tier. Job smart is what an employer should be looking for, so it can be a big gamble to hire a high GPA college student who does not have significant work experience, demanding a high price.

B-players are not quite as results-driven as A-players. They see what the A-players can accomplish, but they don't have the aptitude (talent, ability), are not willing to do the work or won't put in the time that is required to get those results.

It is not the case that B-players are not as smart as A-players. Some B-players are smarter than some A-players; they just don't work as effectively. Things may have come easy for them in the past, they may just have passive personalities, or they are not motivated to change their station in life. They may have relied on their intelligence, not hard work, to be at the top and didn't have to fight for the top spots.

I call this "a big fish in a small pond." If a smart person hasn't needed to fight to succeed, what would drive them to get even better? A bigger pond would be one with more talented fish. This may be a higher ranked school, or a company that is known for hiring A-players. That formerly top performer becomes a B-Player in the bigger pond.

C-players do not stand out. They don't do great work, and they don't do bad work. If the company is large enough, there are positions that could be OK for C-players. These could be called Minions. They cost less and can get the job done, as long as the expectations are not too high, and passion for the job is not necessary.

I would caution that C-players (and worse, D-Players if you have any) will have a negative effect on your business, unless there is a physical or effective virtual wall between the top performers.

Passion and motivation are the energy that drives a business. People who are just there for a job will sap energy from others.

* * *

Low performers underserve key customers, attract other low performers, undermine customer loyalty, erode employee morale and trust, fail to proactively find great opportunities, fail to execute, waste money, and repel high performing employees.

* * *

Part of my story may help illustrate this. I grew up in a poor blue collar town in the middle of New Hampshire. New Hampshire has a lot to offer (no income or sales taxes, beautiful surroundings, lakes, ocean, mountains, Presidential candidate visits, etc.) but the education system is not one of its strengths. I attended the most advanced courses in my high school, and I was near the top of my class.

I applied and was accepted into the Electrical Engineering program at the University of New Hampshire in Durham, NH, the flagship of the NH state college system. I felt pretty good about myself. I seemed to fit in on a personal level with many of my freshman classmates not only from New Hampshire, but from other states, primarily Massachusetts.

My wakeup call occurred after the first round of tests in Calculus and Physics. I found that the education others received in high school was far superior to my own. Many told me that the content on the tests for them was all review, yet I was seeing much of the material for the first time. Needless to say, I was no longer at the top of the class.

I had two other friends from my high school who were in the mechanical engineering program who experienced the same. One dropped out freshman year, and the other transferred out sophomore year to an easier school. But I did not. I stayed and clawed my way out of the hole I was in.

I came from a small pond, and this was a much bigger pond – with 16 thousand students, maybe it was more of a lake. I found that there were much higher IQ fish, and even they were challenged by the engineering curriculum. It was hard to fathom at the time that there were even bigger lakes of more talented fish, namely private colleges with bigger, well-known names and tougher entry criteria in the New England area.

Electrical Engineering is a difficult major, and pure theory was never my strength. I found that I excelled in applying knowledge to real world situations. I had a few internships that helped me understand that. I was fortunate that one of my interviewers at a college employment fair recognized that my value was more than my GPA, and ended up recommending me to my future employer.

Although many had higher GPAs, few had my hands on experience. I was hired into a big pond (Raytheon Company), and soon stood out among the many that were hired at the same time. I worked alongside others from "better" schools, but I think the reason I excelled was because I worked harder to become job smart.

While it was a big pond, after less than 5 years, I felt that I did not fit the culture. I found that there were too many C-players for me, and I wanted to challenge myself further. I won't get into details here, but I found that the engineering technicians who were in a union did not push themselves to the level that I thought was needed to deliver a successful project. (One example: one person told me to slow down because I was making others look bad.)

While I had made many friends there (I was president of the golf league – a great way to bond with the lab manager), I felt I needed more. I had to make a decision: stay and relax my standards, or try to find a place that was the right fit for me. I reached for an opportunity at a company with tough hiring standards.

The company's hiring process was nicknamed the "walk of fire" because the interview process was so challenging. They had some of their smartest people on the interview team. Synopsys, Inc. (SNPS) hired me more for my EQ (Emotional Quotient, or Emotional Intelligence) than IQ, and more for my tenacity, temperament, work smarts, and experience than for my GPA and Alma Mater.

At Synopsys, I worked with some of the smartest and most talented people I have ever met in my life, yet I was still able to excel and lead a team that was smarter on a measured scale (IQ, GPA, etc.) than I was. The company culture was one of continual improvement, and I thrived in that environment.

The moral of the story is that A-players don't come from a cookie cutter. It is their results that matter. Some people are born smart, and some are a product of a challenging environment. Some people challenge themselves, and others respond well in an organization with high expectations. A-players don't play it safe. A-players rise to the challenge.

Look at a candidate's past to see where she was challenged and how she responded. Look at the resume for continuous improvement, and verify the information through the interview process. Interviewers need to ask about personal results (not team results).

Don't settle for B-players or C-players. Your organization's A-players need peers. A-players can spot other A-players, and they tend to respect and associate with one another. A-players attract other A-players, and B-players attract and prefer to hire C-players because it makes the B-player feel like an A-player. That is why you want your A-players on your interview team.

Another thing to consider is that B and C-players tend to become subservient to or report to the A-players.

We can compare A-players to wolves. As a pack, they are a force that can triumph over even larger animals (in other words, a big challenge). But what of a lone wolf? Wolves prefer to live in packs, and achieve together. A lone wolf will try to find a pack because they don't do as well on their own. If there isn't a pack of A-players at your company, the A-players you do have will leave to find a pack at another company.

* * *

Don't settle for B-players or C-players.

* * *

This book will give you a process that works, is scalable, and promises that you can hire a great team. It still takes work – you have to put in the effort. Taking the easy way out or cutting corners is rarely successful.

Chapter 2: Determine Openings

Before you decide to hire another person, ask yourself these questions:

- Do you really need to hire for this position? Is there a long-term need for the position?
- Is someone in the wrong place in the company who can fit this need? Is the needed skill set available?
- Can you restructure/shuffle current employees to cover the tasks of this position?
- Can it be done by a part time person? Is part-time the right answer?
- Can it be done more economically by a contractor? (Usually this is not a core function of the company, e.g. bookkeeping or marketing.)
- What will be the return on the investment? (i.e. Will you bring in more than you pay out?)

How do you know when it is time to hire a person? You are probably worried about taking on more expense, but you also don't want to lose revenue by not having the right people. So how do you determine it is time to hire? Here are some signs that it is the right time:

Everyone is swamped

It is probably time to hire someone when everyone has too much to do. I'm not talking about things that they could do if they had time. I'm talking about not having enough time to complete the things they need to complete by a due date without working excessive hours.

While working a lot of hours is OK in the short term, working too many hours has many negatives over the long term. At a minimum, it can lead to high stress and poor decision making. Working long hours for an extended period can cause burnout and employee dissatisfaction that can lead to a decline in customer care and unwanted employee attrition. Typically your A-players leave first because they are in demand by other companies. It is those who can't find something easily that are left when the best leave.

Typically a manager will hear complaints if people are overworked. Investigate this further before deciding, because some employees just like to complain. If there is legitimately more work that they can handle, you may not need to hire someone new – just manage your current employees differently. (That last sentence is obviously from a business advisor and not a recruiter.)

You are leaving money on the table

If there are high margin jobs that you are turning down, it is time to hire. Before you do, consider cutting out the low margin jobs. As you grow, fire the bottom 5-10% of your clients as measured by margin. (This is not just those who want to pay less, but also those who require lots of resources and support.) If your margins are good, hire people who can bring in the revenue that would have gone to another company.

I worked with a company that had growing pains, and much of it was due to the CEO not being able to let go and delegate to competent people. This is a legitimate issue: sometimes it is hard to transfer enough knowledge to others to make them proficient quickly enough. With that said, it is an issue that can be solved with good management.

Many times if the CEO says, "I want to stay small," or "our culture will change," or "our customer care will suffer," this is fear of growing too fast for the management to catch up. Many times, a seasoned advisor or manager is needed.

More revenue can solve a lot of problems, and sometimes a company needs to achieve "critical mass" to be sustainable. An example of this is a low margin provider that can only prosper with a little from many.

In technical terms, a critical mass is the smallest amount of fissile material needed for a sustained nuclear fission chain reaction - any less and the reaction stops. (Sorry, it is hard to not think like an engineer.) Before a CEO decides to remain a boutique company, talk to a business advisor to mentor and help manage the risk of growth.

You will save money

It may be counterintuitive to think that you can save money by hiring. Another person means more benefits, additional payroll expenses, more office equipment (computer, desk, chair, phone), and the time and expense required to hire and onboard someone new. But overtime for hourly workers can be expensive, and that can apply to salaried exempt employees as well. (A new law on this was passed in 2016, but was being suspended by a judge in Texas at the time of this writing.)

Just be careful that the employees understand that hiring another is a good idea. In some cases they may not. One example is the impact of hiring more police in a small town. The police union specifies the working conditions and compensation. Typically police can work 8, 10 or 12 hour shifts with a few days off between. I know many police officers work their entrepreneurial businesses on their days off, but they can also fill that time by covering for another officer, off-duty privately paid traffic details, and other event details.

More police officers means more competition for this extra income that could be time and a half or double time if paid by the municipality. Hiring more police officers would save money if the overtime is being paid consistently. I can tell you firsthand that the officers would rather have the overtime pay that can add 30+% to their household income.

The job generates income

It is usually easy to decide to add salespeople. Once you have a proven sales system and onboarding process, adding more proven salespeople just brings in more money (break even in 6+ months) because they tend to be heavily commission based.

While salespeople directly affect revenue, other jobs also increase revenue directly. Hiring anyone who is "billable" (like a consultant or attorney) is usually a good choice if he is not "on the bench," meaning as long as he is working on client work. If the person can be billable quickly, the decision is typically an easy one.

Other indirect revenue producers may also be easy decisions. If you cannot keep up with orders, and it is sustainable, it may be time to hire someone to fix the bottleneck. But don't just hire anyone; hire someone with the appropriate skills that will alleviate the bottleneck.

High ROI

Hiring an "overhead" position is a harder choice. An overhead position is one that does not contribute to increasing the revenue.

Administrators, human resources and maintenance employees are examples of overhead, and you need to look for a return on investment (ROI) on a permanent position.

Typically I recommend hiring contractors for things that are not core competencies for your business. HR contractors are common for small businesses because you don't need HR help all the time, but when you do, it is great to have an experienced professional available. Administrators are the tougher positions to decide upon hiring.

My recommendation is to hire administrative help if that help will free up a revenue producing person to be more effective. For the solopreneur looking to grow, I recommend getting a great assistant who will complement the abilities of the founder and offload the non-revenue producing work. For a sales group that has to do all their own documentation, I recommend getting help that allows the salespeople to do what they are uniquely qualified to do; find and close more clients.

Maximize the value of a productive, well-compensated executive/employee by taking the administrative tasks (ex. bookkeeping, logistical, clerical, reporting) off of her plate. The ROI should be high.

Create a new position

To put this in a context that will make sense, consider how filing is done (whether electronic or paper) as an analogy. Typically information needs to be "filed," so a folder is created and the information is added to it. Then when related information needs to be filed, it is put into the same folder, and this continues until the folder gets big or unwieldy. Once it gets so big that it takes too long to find the information you want quickly, either a new folder or sub-folder is created and a group of more tightly related information is put into the new folder. Creating new positions should happen in the same way.

When a company is small, employees typically wear many hats and the founder may be referred to the "chief cook and bottle-washer." Everyone chips in where needed. As a company grows, positions become more specialized. Once an employee has to wear too many important hats (like having too much information in the folder), a new position (or folder) needs to be created. The most important or best mastered tasks continue to be done by the person, and the rest is taken off of her plate. In doing so, always consider if these are related skills that a new hire could easily bring if the position is vacated.

There may already be someone in the company who has the talent and time to pick up the tasks, but in a growing company, it could be better to create a new position to focus on the tasks that have been shucked off. Staffed by someone with the skills to do these tasks, the new position can make these formerly low priority tasks stand out to help the company, and the seasoned employee's retained tasks get more attention and renewed focus.

I once had a client who ran a health club. The Membership Services (sales) people not only sold memberships to prospective clients, but also handled members' questions and concerns. I recommended that the two major tasks be separated for many reasons:

1. Good salespeople are hard to find, so it is better to leverage their unique talents (lead generation and closing) and leave the rest to another department.
2. Focusing the salespeople on proactive tasks rather than reactive issues results in continuous sales flow.
3. There are many more customer service type people who can handle members' concerns (and are likely more empathetic) to provide a satisfactory resolution.

4. The cost of a customer service person is lower than a good salesperson, so why spend more on a function than you need to?

Taking the reactive tasks off the plate of the sales staff not only brought clarity in roles, but also brought better results to both positions.

Watch out for...

Whether you agree or disagree with the labor laws, certain laws kick in when companies get to a certain size (10, 20, or 50 employees for example). These laws include Family and Medical Leave, Parental Leave, Medical Insurance, COBRA, and others. Also, individual states can make the laws more stringent, so know your local laws.

For instance, many years ago, Massachusetts required companies to provide health insurance if they had 11 employees or more, but then the Affordable Care Act raised that to 50 employees or more. This will likely change again if it is replaced with another policy.

Part-time vs. Full-time

For small businesses, I recommend looking seriously at part-time employees for administrative jobs and short term needs.

Benefits of part-time employees:

- Great talent is often untapped.
  - I have had great results by hiring stay-at-home moms for administrative jobs (bookkeeping is a great example). In many cases they are

overqualified, know how to get things done quickly, and have the ability to multitask.

- o There are times in life when people need to work part time instead of full time. I have seen this happen for a year or two when an elderly parent needs care. As above, there are very competent people who can easily handle the administrative job.
- o One client hired an Olympic athlete for times that fit around training hours.
- o College students can often work after or between classes, but just be aware that academics will likely come before their job.

- Employers don't have to pay benefits if employee works under 20 hours/week. This is true everywhere, and in some places the limit is over 30 hours.
- Hours can provide great scheduling flexibility.
  - o Many of those mentioned under #1 can work outside of regular hours.
- Don't have to overpay when not a full-time need. When the part-time person moves on, you may then have a need for full-time and can find the right person.
- If part-time people make up a full time position, losing one leaves much less than a 40 hour gap to fill.

Potential negatives to part-time employees:

- The commitment (and maybe passion) is not present.
  - o The job is likely not the employee's life goal.
  - o A better paying, more flexible, or more local job can draw your part-timer away.
  - o When life circumstances change, employee will move on.
- They may have less knowledge of the job.

- o Lack of time and consistency in the job prevents depth of knowledge.
  - o If the job is seasonal, the person could have been away from the job for months, and may not come back.
  - o It takes longer than a full time employee to become proficient due to fewer hours per week.
  - o The part time employee may have been hired for her incredible potential, but she may not have the experience doing this kind of job before.
- You may not find the competency you desire.
  - o Some jobs require depth of experience, and that may be hard to find in a part-timer.
  - o The ideal candidate is not doing an online search that includes the words "part-time," so your position may not be seen by those with the desired skills.

If you can afford to hire a full-time employee, it is probably better for a growing company. Caution: don't try to lowball the compensation if you can't afford to pay the full-time market rate because you'll get what you pay for – something less than an A-player. A part-time employee can be a great fit at least in the short term. Just don't shortcut the hiring process because it is a part-time position.

Now that you've determined you need to hire someone, for what job are you hiring?

Some job titles may say secretary, marketer, or administrator, but exactly what will the person be doing? What is it that the new employee needs to do that someone else can't do? What kind of experience is necessary in order to succeed in this job?

Note: do use plain English in the job description. Don't use a title like "Queen of Awesomeness" if you are looking for an HR Director. Use the wording that someone would use in a Google Search.

This is where a great job description comes in. The job description should motivate A-players. It should say "What success looks like." We'll dive into this in the following chapters.

Summary & Action Items

Do you really need to hire for this position?

- Is someone in the wrong place in the company who can fit this need?
- Can you restructure/shuffle current employees to cover the tasks of this position?
- Can it be done by a part time person?
- Can it be done more economically by a contractor?
- What will be the return on the investment?

Signs you need to make a hire:

- Everyone is swamped with too much work
- You are leaving money on the table
- You will save money
- The job generates income
- High ROI
- Create a new position
- Watch out for labor laws!

Part-time vs. Full-time

Now that you've determined you need to hire someone, for what job are you hiring?

Chapter 3: The Process

The Perfect Hire Blueprint process is a logical, step by step, linear process. While the process has been condensed successfully in some cases (I don't recommend this), it has been proven to work in many companies and for many different positions. The process has been used to hire positions such as sales, marketing, admin, CPA, membership services, fitness trainers, front desk greeters, engineers and other tech positions, and managerial positions such as COO.

The process solves the overall issue: How do I hire the right person when the resume and cover letter are written by experts, the candidate is coached on how to interview, the references won't tell me the real scoop, and headhunters cost too much?

Here is a one-page view of the process:

	Step	Problem	Description/Solution	Transformational Benefits
Setup	Step 1 Profile/Benchmark	Who is the ideal candidate and what behavior, values, and skills are needed?	Stakeholders determine why the job exists. Each takes an assessment to create an ideal candidate benchmark.	* Buy-in on ideal candidate * A standard for measuring * Agreement of stakeholders
	Step 2 Job Description/ Ad/Sourcing	What will the person do? How do I reach the ideal person? How do I get enough candidates?	Tell exactly what the job is, and speak directly to the perfect fit. Fish in the right pond.	* Job Function Clarity * Reduces # of bad applicants * Perfect applicants apply
Screen	Step 3 Track and Qualify	How do I track all the people and their info? How do I filter it down to just the best?	Use a system to track all applicants and relevant info. Filter out those not close to the benchmark	* Tracks all candidates * Organizes all information * Communicate with stakeholders * Reduces # of phone screens
	Step 4 Phone Screen	How do I know if this person is a good fit? How can I determine that quickly?	A cursory check to see if the candidate is a possible fit, and if job/company is a fit for candidate	* Efficient way to filter * Saves time and money * Sets expectations
	Step 5 1st Interview	How do I determine if this is the right person without wasting everyone's time?	A team of Behavioral Interviewers with non-overlapping questions. Practical if applicable.	* Get all the info needed * Gives candidate feel for environment * Observe body language
	Step 6 Assessment/ Gap Analysis	How can I get more info that is not written or said by candidate and check what was said and my gut feel?	Science-Based Assessment uncovers strengths and weaknesses. Analysis compares that to the benchmark	* Objective assessment * Deeper than surface * EEOC Compliance
	Step 7 2nd Interview	How do I uncover what we need to know? Can I determine gaps in skill set?	Focus on the gaps between the benchmark and the assessment.	* Fills in the blanks * Create a stronger bond * Raises candidate excitement
	Step 8 Other Requirements	How can I confirm the candidate meets all the requirements?	Reference checks, background check, transcripts, physical, certifications needed	* Reduces surprises * Reduces liability * Confirms if qualified
Secure	Step 9 Job Offer	How do I know what is a good (yet affordable) offer that will motivate the candidate?	An excited applicant accepts a reasonable offer. Now what will be accepted?	* Will not have to overpay * Will have a motivated employee
	Step 10 Post Offer Actions	Now that the offer is made and accepted, how do I know if the person will show up?	Walk her through all the decision steps: definitive decision, giving notice, telling people, preparing.	* Helps ensure the candidate shows up on the first day feeling eager and energized.
	Step 11 Onboarding	For a comprehensive Onboarding guide, visit perfecthireblueprint.com/onboarding		

To download this grid, visit PerfectHireBlueprint.com/Resources

Overview of the Process

There are 11 steps above in the grid for a snapshot of the Perfect Hire Blueprint. Here are all the steps in summary and then we'll dive into each:

Part 1: Setup

1. Job opening is determined.
2. Profile/Benchmark for position is created.
3. Job description is created and pay structure is determined.
4. Approval to hire is obtained.
5. Interview team is determined (your A-players) and roles are defined.
6. Ad is created and pushed to all sourcing channels (if necessary, recruiters are contracted).

Part 2: Screen

7. Leads come in from all sources and all are entered into tracking software.
8. Leads are either filtered and sent to hiring manager or are sent directly to hiring manager without qualification depending on department.
9. Hiring manager or screener reviews the candidate's information and determines if phone/video screen is warranted.
10. Candidates that don't make the grade are informed that the company does not see a good match.
11. If phone screen goes well, hiring manger (may have help of assistant) schedules interview with candidate and with team of interviewers.
12. The day of the interview, the candidate meets with each interviewer.

13. Assessment is taken and Gap Analysis is created.
14. Assessment Analysis is provided to the hiring manager.
15. Hiring manger has second interview to follow up on issues raised during first visit and by the Assessment.
16. A roundtable is convened to confirm which candidate, if any, is qualified.
17. Hiring manger determines if offer is to be made and creates offer letter (may have admin help).

Part 3: Secure

18. Approved offer is presented to candidate.
19. Offer acceptance procedures are followed to insure new hire shows up on first day.
20. Onboarding.

This might look like a lot of steps, but this book is about finding the Perfect Hire. If you follow the process, you will get the Perfect Hire. If you skip one or multiple steps, the surety of the process drops. You may be able to find great employees by doing only a few of the steps, but if you want a repeatable process that consistently places the right people in the right seats to help grow your company, and reduce the required management oversight, this process could be exactly what you need.

If you are worried that this is too much for your business or that it takes too long, all of this can happen very fast, and it needs to. I recommend that you move quickly no matter the environment. When there are 100+ people for every job opening (such as what happened in the US in 2010-2012), the hiring company is in control. Since there aren't enough jobs to go around, candidates are more tolerant of a company that moves slowly and makes them jump through hoops.

When there are fewer candidates for each job (as is the case in a growing economy), the control shifts to the A-players. If a company does not have a smooth, less demanding application and interview process, the A-players will move on to good companies that do move quickly and offer a growth path. But of course, if the company has a reputation of only hiring A-players, an A-player will do what is needed to get hired.

Selling an Interview Candidate

"Selling" your company to an interview candidate is incredibly important to keep in mind during the entire hiring process.

At the time of this writing the labor market is tightening (at or near all-time low unemployment). There are fewer candidates applying for each job, and there are fewer good candidates who are actively looking. The best candidates will have more opportunities than just your company. There may be times when you won't even be able to find any minimally qualified candidates, never mind A-players. My advice is not to settle, but to keep searching.

This is why getting the candidate excited about your company is critically important. It is a seller's market, and the seller is putting a higher price on her high demand skills. If you are going to get the best people to say yes to your company, you need to do more than just wait until the offer to see if the candidate is interested.

You should be selling the benefits of your company early in the process.

If the candidate wants to work for your company:

- the process goes faster (he returns calls and his schedule is more flexible),
- you are less likely to get into a salary auction (bidding wars are brutal),

- the offer does not have to be the best in order to get him to accept, and
- you won't get that call after the offer is accepted saying he took another job or he wants another concession.

If the candidate is indifferent about your company:

- the person tends to drag his feet to allow other companies to compete (this could also include the company at which he is currently employed),
- he doesn't appear to be totally engaged in the conversation or interview (read the body language),
- the candidate just disappears; no longer able to be reached by phone or email,
- your offer will be just the starting point for the negotiation, and
- he will find minor reasons why the job is not ideal (commute is 5 minutes longer, traffic is worse, daycare is in the other direction, etc.).

Here's what you need to do to sell your company and the position during the process:

1. The ad and job description need to highlight WHY someone should work for your company. Asking current employees why they work there is the best way to get the real reasons, rather than the key reasons perceived by management.

2. Every interaction should "sell" a little. Even emails to candidates should include an "about us" at the end as to why the company is a great place to work. Use employee testimonials, point them to your LinkedIn company page or reference Glassdoor.com if the reviews are good. 3rd

party sources are viewed as more credible because they are hard to manipulate.

3. Interviews need to be part selling and part information gathering. An interview is a two-way street: you are interviewing her, and she is interviewing you.

- The amount of selling depends on how difficult it is to get good candidates to apply. In a down market, you may have hundreds of applicants, and selling is less important. In a booming market, there may be fewer A-players applying for the job. In that case, about 30-40% of the time you should be discussing the benefits of the company, and the opportunities for learning and career growth.
- Have your A-players on the interview team. They will attract other A-players by showing their aptitude, responsibilities and commitment.
- The manager/leader the candidate works for is an important part of the candidate's decision. It's important for that personal connection to be formed.

4. At the end of the second interview, the hiring manager should ask this question: "If we offered you the job today, would you say yes today?" If the answer is not yes, then ask, "What would go into your decision making?"

- This helps you gauge whether the person would take an offer, or whether you need to address any concerns before making the offer.
- In all but very small companies, the offer needs to be approved by at least one superior. Sweetening the deal after an offer is made will require another

round of signoff. Don't go back to ask for more — uncover what will be needed before the offer is approved.

5. When making the offer, sell the position, the company, and the difference the person will make for the company and for their career.

    If you think the candidate is ready to take the offer, it's time to talk about compensation. This will set up the candidate to be less focused on the money and more on the big picture. If the body language isn't open and friendly, you are likely setting yourself up for a post-offer negotiation.

    - After the offer is made, the power shifts to the candidate. The company has shown their cards, but the candidate has not yet shown her cards. To make a poker analogy: if you feel you have the best hand, you try to make the pot as large as possible before you show your cards.
    - After the offer is made, some candidates feel it is now time to ask for what they really want (because the power has shifted). If you uncover any issues with an offer or special considerations before the offer is made, then the process is positive for everyone.
        - One person I hired needed to be relocated a good distance. His hobby was woodworking. His relocation allowance had to be significantly increased to move his workshop consisting of table saw, lathe, band saw, planer, etc.

- The person making the offer needs to have a contingency budget when making the offer. It is best to close the negotiation at that time, rather than allow it to drag on.
  - The offer should be able to be reconfigured and stay within the contingency budget.
  - If the candidate is allowed to leave without a deal, he may ask others, "They want me! What else should I ask for?"

You have interviewed many people by this time. You are offering the job to the best candidate you have met. If the candidate does not accept, it will take more time and money to find another candidate (refer to Chapter 1: Preparing to Hire, What are the Costs of Hiring?).

Now let's dive deep into the process.

Section 1: Setup & Pre-hire

Chapter 4: Profile/Benchmark

As I've stated before, a significant key to hiring success is the online Assessment portion of the process.

Personal preferences and biases show up first in the job description. We picture someone who succeeded in the role and strive for the same type, or we remember someone who failed and try to get the opposite. This does not create a predictive process for hiring success. If the job description is not right, then how does someone who perfectly matches the description succeed in the job?

The Benchmark Assessment or Job Profile (see PerfectHireBlueprint.com/Resources for examples) must be the starting point for all hiring. While it's possible to hire well without it, the chance of success is much lower. If you've hired a Mis-fit, you know the pain and expense involved to shed that person – not even accounting for the expense and time required in the hiring process, and the opportunity cost of not having the right person.

The Job Profile is the standard by which a candidate should be measured, and the Job Benchmark Assessment is the key to the perfect hire.

But wait a minute. You've said that all I need is A-players and I'll be fine. Why don't you just tell me how to get an A-player? Why do I need a Job Profile or Benchmark?

While A-players do share some traits, every job still needs a minimum skill set. An A-player salesperson would not have the same top 10 skills as an A-player accountant or actuary. The Profile will identify the key skills needed for the particular role.

The difference between a Profile and a Benchmark is that the Benchmark uses an extensive online Multi-respondent Job Questionnaire, while the Profile is less rigorous (and more prone to mistakes). These two pieces work together to create a much more detailed and effective job description.

The Job Profile is likely a Word document, which is the result of a facilitated process, and the Job Report (or Benchmark) is a PDF generated by the online Assessment system that should be referenced when creating the Job Profile.

The Benchmark Assessment will determine the ideal candidate for the job. Stakeholders (who may include company owners, managers, and selected employees) will complete a Benchmark Job Assessment to determine the qualities necessary or desired in candidates.

- 3-6 people are involved in the Benchmark. These are the stakeholders - those that are currently in or are in close contact with position
- Vital Responsibilities are created that are specific to the job as identified by the stakeholders
- Stakeholders help create the Multi-respondent Job Report (online Assessment)
- Interview questions are created by Benchmark (Job Report)
- Full Benchmark binder is created (recommended, but not required)

A Job Benchmark will help determine whether a candidate has the desired qualities necessary to be successful in the position.

With an accurate Benchmark, the job description will be more than just a list of duties. The Benchmark forms the job description and the ad that will be seen by prospective employees. It is the starting point that helps ensure that the right candidate is hired.

To create this Benchmark we need to know why this job is different from other positions in the company:

- Why is this job needed?

- What are the responsibilities that are unique to this position?

Once these questions are answered, the Benchmark gives an outline of the ideal candidate.

* * *

No matter your hiring process, the Benchmark and the Personal Assessment will improve your hiring success rate dramatically. We have found that in over 90% of the cases using this process, new hires stay at least a year.

* * *

Step 1: Perfect Hire Profile (Avatar)

Avatar is more than a popular movie. The definition that I'm using from Webster's dictionary is: "someone who represents a type of person, an idea, or a quality." An avatar, in marketing, is used to determine the traits of the ideal customer:

- Where does he live?
- How does he dress?
- What kind of car does he drive?
- What is his age?
- What is the family's income?

For hiring, this definition is good as we are looking for a specific "type" of person. **It is much easier to find the perfect hire if you first know what behaviors, values and skills you are looking for.**

I know some companies say that they want candidates with a high IQ, high energy, and a great conversationalist, and they tailor their interview questions to uncover those traits. **I don't believe that you can say that these traits are important for every employee in a company.**

For instance, some employees may be behind the scenes. Looking for a good cultural fit could span all positions, but individual behavioral traits are not one-size-fits-all.

The ideal first step is to create a perfect hire profile for the position. As mentioned earlier, this involves 3-6 stakeholders in a room together answering two questions:

1. Why this job is different than any of the other jobs?
2. Why is this position needed?

There needs to be a good explanation why no other position is right for doing this work. The right people to contribute and answer these questions might be:

- the manager of the position,
- the most successful person doing the job (definition of success is up to the manager), and
- the people who will interact with this position most.

By asking why the job is unique and needed, it takes the mind off who we think the ideal person would be (we'd have someone in mind), and focus on what is really required. What we are looking for is not the typical job description.

Profile of a Perfect Hire

The perfect hire will have some combination of the following Behaviors, Motivators and Soft Skills. The desired amount of each is determined through the Benchmarking process, and the Job Report will identify which of the following are most important. Here are the alphabetically ordered lists of what we might look for:

Behaviors (DISC)

Your observable behavior and related emotions contribute to your success on the job. When matched to the job, they play a large role in enhancing your performance.

1. **Analysis of Data** - Information is maintained accurately for repeated examination as required.
2. **Competitiveness** - Tenacity, boldness, assertiveness and a "will to win" in all situations.
3. **Consistency** - The ability to do the job the same way.
4. **Customer Relations** - A desire to convey your sincere interest in them.
5. **Frequent Change** - Moving easily from task to task or being asked to leave several tasks unfinished and easily move on to the new task with little or no notice.
6. **Frequent Interaction with Others** - Dealing with multiple interruptions on a continual basis, always maintaining a friendly interface with others.
7. **Following Policy** - Complying with the policy or if no policy, complying with the way it has been done.
8. **Follow Up and Follow Through** - A need to be thorough.
9. **Organized Workplace** - Systems and procedures followed for success.
10. **People Oriented** - Spending a high percentage of time successfully working with a wide range of people from diverse backgrounds to achieve "win-win" outcomes.
11. **Urgency** - Decisiveness, quick response and fast action.

12. **Versatility** - Bringing together a multitude of talents and a willingness to adapt the talents to changing assignments as required.

Driving Forces (Motivators)

To create engagement and superior job performance it is important to align the individual's driving forces with the rewards of the job. Each pair is at different ends of the same scale. If someone is high in the first, they tend to be low in the second and vice versa.

1. **Theoretical**
    a. **Intellectual** - People who are driven by opportunities to learn, acquire knowledge and the discovery of truth.
    b. **Instinctive** - People who are driven by utilizing past experiences, intuition and seeking specific knowledge when necessary.
2. **Utilitarian**
    a. **Resourceful** - People who are driven by practical results, maximizing both efficiency and returns for their investments of time, talent, energy and resources.
    b. **Selfless** - People who are driven by completing tasks for the greater good, with little expectation of personal return.
3. **Aesthetic**
    a. **Harmonious** - People who are driven by the experience, subjective viewpoints and balance in their surroundings.
    b. **Objective** - People who are driven by the functionality and objectivity of their surroundings.
4. **Social**

   a. **Altruistic** - People who are driven by the benefits
       they provide others.
   b. **Intentional** - People who are driven to assist
       others for a specific purpose, not just for the sake of
       being helpful or supportive.
5. **Individualistic**
   a. **Commanding** - People who are driven by status,
       recognition and control over personal freedom.
   b. **Collaborative** - People who are driven by being in
       a supporting role and contributing with little need
       for individual recognition.
6. **Traditional**
   a. **Structured** - People who are driven by traditional
       approaches, proven methods and a defined system
       for living.
   b. **Receptive** - People who are driven by new ideas,
       methods and opportunities that fall outside a
       defined system for living.

Soft Skills (Competencies)

While some of these may look similar to the behavioral (DISC)
traits above, they are assessed differently and can identify
someone who has adapted to a natural behavioral weakness.

There are 25 Competencies that help determine if the candidate is
a good fit:

1. **Appreciating Others** - Identifying with and caring about
    others.
2. **Conceptual Thinking** - The ability to analyze
    hypothetical situations or abstract concepts to compile
    insight.

3. **Conflict Management** - Addressing and resolving conflict constructively.
4. **Continuous Learning** - Taking initiative in learning and implementing new concepts, technologies and/or methods.
5. **Creativity and Innovation** - Creating new approaches, designs, processes, technologies and/or systems to achieve the desired result.
6. **Customer Focus** - Anticipating, meeting and/or exceeding customer needs, wants and expectations.
7. **Diplomacy** - The ability to treat others fairly, regardless of personal biases or beliefs.
8. **Decision Making** - Utilizing effective processes to make decisions.
9. **Employee Development/Coaching** - Facilitating and supporting the professional growth of others.
10. **Flexibility** - Agility in adapting to change.
11. **Futuristic Thinking** - Imagining, envisioning, projecting and/or predicting what has not yet been realized.
12. **Goal Orientation** - Setting, pursuing and attaining goals, regardless of obstacles or circumstances.
13. **Influencing Others** - Personally affecting others' actions, decisions, opinions or thinking.
14. **Interpersonal Skills** - Effectively communicating, building rapport and relating well to all kinds of people.
15. **Leadership** - Achieving extraordinary business results through people.
16. **Negotiation** - Facilitating agreements between two or more parties.
17. **Personal Accountability** - A measure of the capacity to be answerable for personal actions.
18. **Planning and Organizing** - Utilizing logical, systematic and orderly procedures to meet objectives.
19. **Problem Solving** - Defining, analyzing and diagnosing key components of a problem to formulate a solution.

20. **Project Management** - Identifying and overseeing all resources, tasks, systems and people to obtain results
21. **Resiliency** - The ability to quickly recover from adversity.
22. **Self-Starting** - Demonstrating initiative and willingness to begin working.
23. **Teamwork** - Working effectively and productively with others.
24. **Time and Priority Management** - Demonstrating self-control and an ability to manage time and priorities.
25. **Understanding Others** - Understanding the uniqueness and contributions of others.

This is where an additional Assessment, Acumen, comes in. High scores here help solidify the opinion that you have identified an A-player.

The Acumen Assessment uncovers whether a candidate can assess situations and performance, and make good decisions on external factors. It also does the same internally to determine if he can understand, decide and control his actions. Broadly, it measures:

A. **How one sees the world around himself.** This view measures clarity and understanding of people, tasks and systems. It could also be looked at in terms of feeling, doing and thinking from an external standpoint. They are:
   a. Understanding Others
   b. Practical Thinking
   c. Systems Judgment
B. **How one sees himself.** This view measures clarity and understanding of himself, his roles in life and his direction for the future. The internal dimensions are a reflection of himself from both personal and professional viewpoints. They are:
   a. Sense of Self
   b. Role Awareness

c. Self-Direction

When a candidate scores low in these areas, it could indicate an issue being masked, or that he is already at the top end of his potential. Conversely, when someone scores high in these areas, they have the potential to become more than they are. These people could be your next leaders and the key to your succession planning.

Step 2: Determine Vital Responsibilities

The 3-6 stakeholders will determine what the unique requirements (Vital Responsibilities) are for this job. What is required for someone to succeed in this position? Brainstorm the reason, group the responses by similarity, and then prioritize the groups. This will help you determine what responsibilities are vital.

This step may be the most important because it gets all the stakeholders to agree on what is vital. I highly recommend that each stakeholder completes the Job Assessment to gather this information.

Note: I have facilitated groups larger than 6 because there was a desire for inclusion. The resulting Benchmark would have been virtually the same if the Benchmark was built with any 3 of the 6. Also, at least 3 are important because the third breaks the tie between the first 2. After the 4th Assessment, adding additional input rarely makes a significant difference in the Benchmark. The main reason is that those taking the Job Assessment are referring to the Vital Responsibilities that the group agreed to in the facilitated session.

Step 3: Building the Benchmark

While it is possible to find a perfect hire without a Benchmark, I strongly recommend one. Steps 1 and 2 can enable some consensus, but it is hard to implement consistently.

The Benchmark is created with each stakeholder taking a Job Assessment – that is an Assessment on what is needed for the job. They refer to the Vital Responsibilities document that was created with the input from all the stakeholders. This ensures that everyone is on the same page for what is needed for the position.

The Assessment will take between 15-35 minutes depending on how many disciplines make up the Benchmark (it can assess between 2 and 4 disciplines).

After everyone completes the Assessment, the results are merged into the multi-user talent report, and the Benchmark uses the average score of the group to identify the desired behavior, drivers, and soft skills that are the most important for the Perfect Hire. If there are outliers that would skew the results, the specifics are inspected to see if the results should be included or excluded.

Now you have the Avatar for the position. This report not only describes what the ideal candidate looks like, but it also provides interview questions to extract the information needed to find the right person.

Why is a Benchmark necessary?

Without an online Job Assessment and using a profile, the hiring process is less dependent on the interpretation of a personal Assessment, and more dependent on human interaction. This means many steps in the process will be more susceptible to human bias. It has been proven that we each have biases that we don't know we have, and it is these biases that lead to Mis-fits. To get the perfect hire, objective data is needed, and Assessments provide that data.

What happens if you do not have a profile? Paraphrasing from Alice in Wonderland, "If you don't know where you're going, any road will get you there." Many people have a rough idea of what they want in a new hire, but without the profile, it is likely that the person hired will not be the right fit for the long term. A vague idea among the interviewers is a bad idea, since everyone will have their own interpretation.

One of my clients hired a candidate who had applied for a sales position. The owner of the company decided that since the candidate had recently finished his MBA, the person offered much more than was needed for the sales position. The owner thought that the candidate might be the right person to get on the bus, but there wasn't an existing seat for him. (The book *Good to Great* tells you to "get the right people on the bus, and get them in the right seats.") A new position needed to be created, and the owner had a rough idea what it might be.

The candidate (let's call him Joe) was very confident in his abilities in virtually every job or subject matter (he referred to himself as a Renaissance man). Joe was hired, but his position was vague, so the other employees didn't know how to interact with him.

Joe was clearly intelligent, and seemed to be given special projects to do. He would talk about high level business topics and wanting to be general manager one day. There was no clear communication and no clear expectations set. Within a year it was evident that Joe had managed to get under the skin of too many people, and the view of these people was that he just didn't fit in.

After paying his salary for a year and getting very little ROI, the owner decided that there wasn't need for Joe's skills. Even

Einstein wouldn't be a good hire if he doesn't fit the company's culture and was not given clear direction. The Perfect Hire Profile specifies the values of the company, and motivators for the position. If these are in alignment, the probability of the perfect hire increases.

Summary & Action Items

Why is a Benchmark necessary?

To take away the human bias and get the perfect hire based on objective data gathered by Assessments

- 3-6 people are involved
- Vital Responsibilities are created
- Job Assessments are taken by stakeholders
- Multi-respondent Benchmark is created
- Interview questions included in the Benchmark
- Full Benchmark binder is created

A Job Benchmark will be the litmus test as to whether a candidate has the desired qualities necessary to be successful in the position.

Why is the position needed?

Step 1: Perfect Hire Profile

Step 2: Determine Vital Responsibilities

Step 3: Building the Benchmark

Chapter 5: Job Description

The job description is an important step. It is critical that all involved understand what the role of the candidate will be. While this should be covered under Benchmarking, this process fleshes out the SOAR Model of HR problem solving:

- **S**ituation or problem to solve
- **O**bstacles to success
- **A**ctions needed
- **R**esults expected

Not only should the job description outline the skills and competencies necessary for the role, but it also defines where a position fits within an organization. It can be used to manage employee performance, as well.

What will this new employee do? Make sure you are very clear about the function of the job – this will help you write the ad, reduce the number of bad applicants and ensure that the right applicants are submitting their resumes for the job.

A good job description includes:

1. The job title
2. Department and Manager (who the person reports to)
3. Responsibilities
4. Qualifications, skills and experience required

Keep the job description concise, clear and conversational.

To see some examples of effective job descriptions, visit PerfectHireBlueprint.com/Resources

Summary & Action Items

A good job description includes:

- The job title
- Department and Manager (who the person reports to)
- Responsibilities
- Qualifications, skills and experience required

Keep the job description concise, clear and conversational.

Chapter 6: Creation of Ad

How to post a great job ad

The job ad is NOT the same as a job description. Think about a soap commercial on TV. Soap is not easy to differentiate, but companies try to appeal to their target audience. Here are some examples:

Ivory	No perfume, and it floats
Dove	Women, moisturizing
Zest	Clean, no filmy feeling
Irish Spring	Men, fresh scent

After all, it is just soap – it would clean anyone. But soap companies know that if you try to appeal to everyone, you will target no one and will not stand out from the crowd. Your job ad needs to stand out, so don't make it generic.

How do I reach the ideal person? How do I get enough candidates? **Tell them exactly what the job is, and speak directly to the perfect fit.** Fish in the right pond to get the right people for the job.

In order to make a good hire, you first need to attract great candidates. Writing a highly targeted ad using the right keywords and phrases will attract more qualified candidates and make the hiring process much smoother.

What separates good ads from average ads is how they are written: the ad should be written to "speak to" your ideal candidate. When the right person reads the ad, he should think, "That is my ideal job." If he thinks that, he is more likely to apply, and also more likely to do any prequalification activities that you require.

You Talkin' to Me?

Your ad should start with WHY. Why should the person work for your company in this position? The Why is the motivator. The Why is the reason your company is in business – not the thing your company does.

The job ad needs to speak to the ideal target candidate, and if this person isn't actively seeking a job change, you may have only one chance to catch her attention. Studies have shown that what the company stands for is as important as the job itself, and this has never been truer than for a company trying to hire Millennials.

As mentioned previously, the Job Profile will tell you what kind of person you are looking for to fill a certain position. Would the person be better suited to the position if he were task oriented or people oriented? Does he love the details, or is he faster paced? Does he value a high return of investment, or does the job require more social awareness?

Even within a company culture, each role will have specific requirements, and the person in the role may need to be motivated differently than the others. What motivates a salesperson might not be what motivates a customer service representative.

For instance, if you are hiring a bookkeeper or controller, you need to attract someone who is detail oriented and who likes to deal with financial matters. The ad might use words like **Careful**, **Cautious**, **Quality**, and a phrase like "**I get it right**." The ideal candidate will be able to relate to these words and phrases easily, as they will be inherent to his personality. In contrast, how many successful sales people do you think would answer an ad like that?

Our experience is that when you write a highly targeted ad, fewer people apply – but more of them are a better fit. This not only saves you time in culling resumes, but also provides a qualified candidate pool.

We recently helped a company hire an inside salesperson. You might think that this would be a typical sales profile, but the Job Profile indicated that we should be hiring a more introverted, process oriented person who will keep making calls and follow a script. The role required that the person not take shortcuts, and also enter the details of all interactions into a Customer Relationship Management (CRM) system.

This role was atypical from an outside salesperson because of the attention to detail and strict adherence to the required process. This is why the Job Profile is crucial to the hiring process.

How do I write the ad?

The Job Ad is a marketing piece. Do not confuse the Ad with the job description. The Ad title does not have to be the title of the position – it should contain the words that your target candidate would search for.

Using the information from the Multi-respondent Job Report and notes from meeting with owners, management, and employees currently in the position, write an ad for the open position. Make sure to reference qualities and skills from Job Report.

Remember that candidates are searching for ads on the job boards – keywords in the title may bring you to the top of their search list. For example, if you are hiring a salesperson and your internal job title is "Customer Advocate," I would include the word "Sales" in the title of the ad because that is likely what is being searched.

The ad is meant to attract the candidates that you want and exclude those who do not meet your requirements. Don't set out the minimum criteria that anyone can meet. The ad should be clear about what a successful candidate looks like.

For instance, the phrases **fast-paced**, **risk taker**, **customer facing**, and **relationship building** would not attract someone who wants to be behind the scenes in support, but a true salesperson may identify with these qualifiers and be attracted to the position.

A successful ad:

- Has a simple, clear, compelling headline:
    - Accounts Payable Specialist – flexible hours & career advancement
    - Health Coach – help our members make positive changes
    - Inside Sales – great work/life balance
- Starts with WHY – paints an exciting vision:
    - Why is your company in business?
    - Why should the candidate want to work for your company?
    - Use phrases such as: "You'll help people..." and "We'll enable...because you..."
- Shares the vital requirements and key performance indicators of the Job Profile:
    - Job description and qualifications
    - Great candidates should be drawn to the job because it just feels right
- Includes WIIFM (what's in it for me)
    - What are the compensation and benefits?
    - How would this enhance their career?

      o   Is it an "all in" job or does it appeal to those seeking work/life balance?
- Challenges the candidate:
  - Gets at the underlying motivations

Come right out and say, "if this job does not speak to your soul, don't apply." Use the information from the Job Report to attract the right personality. Write TO the person you are looking to attract for the position. Tell them exactly what the job is, and speak directly to the perfect fit. You'll attract quality candidates, and heighten your chances of making the perfect hire.

For examples of effective ads, visit
PerfectHireBlueprint.com/Resources

Summary & Action Items

Your ad should start with WHY. Use the information from the Multi-respondent Job Report about what a successful candidate looks like.

A successful ad:

- Has a simple, clear, compelling headline
- Starts with WHY
- Shares the vital requirements and key performance indicators of the Job Profile
- Challenges the candidate
- Tells them WIIFM

Chapter 7: Placement of Ad (Sourcing)

As the competition for great talent and the need to fill positions gets more frantic, the placement of ads is all the more important. You want to carefully consider WHERE your ideal candidate is looking.

Large companies have many openings, so their goal is to get great people to apply for any open position. Even if a candidate is not a perfect fit for a specific job posting, the company wants to keep them engaged until the time when there is a good fit. This includes having their own recruiting events, pushing info out to candidates in a nurturing sequence of information to keep them excited about the company, and engaging in social media.

For the small company that is not hiring constantly, all of these tasks add up to too much overhead. I've compiled this list of what I've found to be the most effective, best "bang-for-your-buck" websites:

Company website:

> Job seekers often have an idea of a certain company to work for, and may have already formed a relationship – either as a customer or with a personal relationship with an employee. The candidate already knows the company, and is interested in applying for a job to work there. By posting directly on your company website, this is the easiest way for interested candidates to see all available openings that may suit them.

> If someone is already passionate about your company, she could make a great hire! Create a page (or ask your web designer) for "Careers at [COMPANY]" so that all of the information is in one place. Make sure your company

culture is clearly defined on this page. Good candidates will check out your website. Your "Careers" page and reasons to work for your company should be easy to find for both candidates and search engines (see Google below).

Industry specific sites:

These tend to find the passive candidates – those that might peek at ads if convenient to see what is happening in the market. If you are looking for someone in the legal field, look to advertise in a legal publication (online and/or offline). The same is true of using trade journals for all licensed professional positions: Accountants, Doctors, Engineers, etc.

Indeed:

Some job listings on Indeed are free to post, but they have recently started charging more to post (usually between $5-10). It uses a pay-per-click method to "boost" your job for more visibility. Indeed is also an aggregator: it pulls jobs from hundreds of sites. One can manage candidates within Indeed, and can send rejection notices (or other notes) quickly and directly to candidates. Indeed is typically the most useful site that we use.

ZipRecruiter:

When you post a job on ZipRecruiter, that job posting is published to 100+ websites (according to their marketing). These include Glassdoor, Jobr, and College Recruiter. Candidates can apply quickly and easily – you can manage them in the ZipRecruiter database, and applications also are emailed directly to the account on file. The benefit of posting to websites such as ZipRecruiter is that you get more people seeing your listing for a flat fee. Their basic account once was $99/month for up to 3 job postings, but that cost has tripled at the time of this writing. Maybe it will be reduced if hiring slows.

Industry specific recruitment sites:

These will vary by industry – they usually will push to a number of other recruiting sites including Indeed. (Examples include: fitnessjobs.com, dice.com)

Craigslist:

Craigslist can be effective for the home services industries or part-time positions, but is not great for more corporate positions. The quality of candidates you receive will depend on the position posted. Since there are so many job-specific websites now, Craigslist isn't used for hiring as much as it was in the past.

LinkedIn:

LinkedIn is an amazing networking tool, depending on your number of contacts. With a big enough list, chances are, at least one of your contacts knows someone (or will reach out to her network) who is in the field you need.

Have your employees create a post for the job opening on their personal profiles to boost visibility.

You should post a "company page" that shares more information about your business. For a fee, you can include a "Careers" tab on the company page to promote job openings. You can also actively recruit LinkedIn members if you have a Recruiter Lite account with job slots, or a premium recruiter account.

Google for Jobs:

> HOLD EVERYTHING! Things just got interesting. Indeed is currently the best place to post a job, and it was one of the best places to look for a job. But in May of 2017, Google announced that its regular search engine will deliver job listings based the searcher's criteria. It knows every website already, so it already has all of the job listings. This will likely have the biggest impact on Indeed and ZipRecruiter, the two biggest aggregators, which charge big money to promote job listings. Google will find the jobs where they are and send the job seeker to the site where it found the listing.

> Google hasn't proven yet that it will dominate, so keep Indeed in your plans for the near future. As an employer, it now makes sense to also focus on a quality posting on your own website. Then go to sites that support your industry. Job seekers who know your industry might go to them, and the rest may just use Google.

If you are planning to use any of these online tools, you may want to create an email alias that forwards to all parties involved, just to keep everything in one place (such as jobs@yourcompany.com). The email alias can also be forwarded to another email address if the recruiting person leaves the company, or the incoming email can go to 2 or more people.

Since hiring tools such as ZipRecruiter and Indeed have a built-in messaging system that hides your real email address, you can communicate via the tool instead of your email. You can also reject unqualified candidates easily through templates in these tools without disclosing any company email addresses.

Referrals:

Often one of the best ways to get good people that fit your company and culture is through referrals. I have found that once you tap into a new vein for good candidates, you want to keep mining that vein. Your best people already know other good people: ask your current employees if they know anyone who would be a good fit for an open position. You could get 50% or more of your best people through your employees' referrals. Your most fruitful list will come from your top employees and new hires. They may know if the person is a fit before they ask.

Networking is also an effective strategy – have your hiring manager and supervisors reach out to their networks to ask if they know anyone who fits the ad (and link to ad). You've already created a great ad, so make sure it is used rather than having employees make up their own description of the job. Have your A-players post the ad on social media.

Referrals can include more than just candidates who are actively looking for a job. If you have something good to offer, those not looking for a job will listen to a trusted friend who talks about the job opening.

Perhaps you could put a referral bonus structure in place for added incentive to find good people. For example, if a referred candidate stays at the company longer than 6 months, the referrer will receive $500. If you are looking to build a long-term team, consider breaking a bigger bonus up into:

1. hire date
2. 6 months
3. 1 year
4. 2 years

You can weight these any way to accomplish your needs, such as

1. 10%
2. 20%
3. 30%
4. 40%

With this structure, they get 60% in the first year, but the referred employee needs to last in order to get the final 40%.

Incentives don't always work – it all depends on what motivates a certain employee and the company culture. If you need to hire many, consider a competition, create teams, and offer a reward for the top referrers.

PHB Tip: Ask new employees if they know other people at their former company who would be a perfect fit for your company. This is a perfect time to ask, while their contacts there are still current. I have successfully "tapped a vein" at one company that produced at least 5 great hires.

A word of caution: Companies may get irritated if your company keeps taking their employees. Remember that laws vary by state, and they can change at any time. I am not aware of any poaching laws, but you may be accused of tortious interference if your poaching tactics include using unproven allegations, ignoring non-compete agreements, or acting in an illegal manner. When sourcing more than a couple of employees or even one key employee from someone in your industry, do yourself a favor and be careful. It is best if you can show that the candidate contacted you first. Headhunters may be asked to shelter your company in these cases, but find someone who will do it for a lower fixed fee if possible, since all the hard work of finding the person is already done.

Outsourced recruiters (headhunters)

There are four acceptable reasons to use headhunters (any combination of these make hiring harder and are also acceptable):

1. You need the person immediately (zero schedule flexibility), your recruiting engine is not currently running, and you are OK with potentially sacrificing long-term retention.
2. You're looking for a needle-in-the-haystack skill set – truly rare to find. You need all options open to you. (ex. MLB Golden-Glove Shortstop that hits >.300)
3. Unemployment (i.e. available talent) is at historical lows and you can't get the employees that you want. As a reference, the 50 year lowest unemployment rate in the US was 3.4%.
4. Hiring from a client/customer. The 3rd party relationship keeps the footsteps from coming directly from your company's front door, enabling you to maintain a good relationship.

If you can't do it all in house, get help with the time consuming tasks, such as crafting an effective job posting, sourcing passive candidates (if needed), culling resumes, and filtering candidates. A well written job ad will receive fewer applicants, but those who do apply will be more targeted, saving hours, if not days, of winnowing candidates.

Once a candidate comes in for an interview, the company needs to own the rest of the process and have the direct relationship. This reduces the amount of leverage for the candidate, allowing the company to steer to a favorable result.

As mentioned before, this is your last resort. Reasons to use a headhunter are:

- money is no object – you want the best talent at all costs
- you need a short term fix
- plausible deniability of poaching
- you are looking for a needle in a haystack
- unemployment rate is at a historical low
- they have a proven track record of sourcing fantastic passive talent

A few other thoughts on using outsourced recruiters:

- They may have no recruit clauses for former clients. This can prevent them from reaching out with new opportunities.
- If you call and ask, "Please send your best [example: Programmers]," these aren't passive candidates.
- Be very clear about what would happen if you are presented with a candidate who is already in your database. (i.e. do you pay them for that candidate?)

Again, I don't think it is necessary for most businesses, but I've put it here for completeness.

Recruiting "Passive" Candidates

Passive candidates are prospective employees who are not actively looking for a new job.

The definition of "active" differs depending on who you ask. For instance, is someone actively looking if he uploads his resume on a recruiting site? Is he actively looking if he clicks on a job ad? If a friend posts an update on LinkedIn about a great company, will he look at the company? I would say these are all passive.

There are many who will always keep their eyes open for better opportunities, but they are not active. Many headhunters say that without using their services, you won't find passive candidates, and that is why I disagree.

You can get these passive candidates without a headhunter. Headhunters can call people who don't look at ads or posts, and who don't upload resumes. They could be fantastic people who could be great for your company but just are not looking. I believe that there are many people who could be great for your company, and many of those will see your ad, posts, and referral notes.

Again, I believe a headhunter who actively calls into businesses is a last resort. If you are going to use one, it should be a fixed rate, exclusive, and you should be presented with a very limited number of candidates who match your needs and have a full write-up. Most times, a good ad in the right places will reach the people you need.

As US unemployment numbers dropped starting in 2015, more was written about passive candidates. Startups are developing software to help find passive candidates, alerting recruiters of changes to a candidate on their watch list. LinkedIn pushed their Recruiter's premium membership to source candidates, which is a lot cheaper than paying commission to a recruiter. Google is quietly introducing a new tool called Google Hire to help employers find great candidates using their algorithm.

This is the intersection of new technology with a good economy. As much as we'd all like to see that last forever, that intersection doesn't happen often. Since 1974, unemployment has only been under 5% three times: during the tech bubble in the late 1990s for a total of ~4 years, and during the housing bubble in the mid-

2000s for ~3 years. We are currently experiencing the same, which also may indicate another unsustainable bubble.

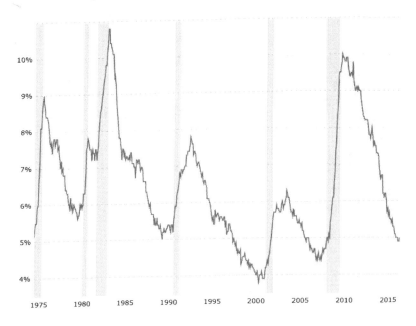

Courtesy Macrotrends.net

PHB TIP: When the unemployment rate falls below 6%, look at the compensation and job satisfaction of your key employees. They have already or will likely get a call from a headhunter. Don't give your key people a reason to return the call. It is much more cost effective to retain a good employee than to go find another and train to the same proficiency. Go to PerfectHireBlueprint.com/Resources for more.

Nurture your candidates

Great candidates aren't always easy to find, so when you find one, you want to keep the communication lines open. Maybe now isn't the best time for a job change for the candidate or a family situation arises that makes change difficult. Stay in touch and don't give her a reason to drop out of the running. Keep your best candidates informed on your hiring progress.

Summary & Action Items

WHERE should you post your ad to find the perfect hire?

- Company website
- Industry specific site
- Indeed
- ZipRecruiter
- Craigslist
- LinkedIn
- Google
- Referrals

Only use a headhunter (outsourced recruiter) IF:

- money is no object
- a short term fix is more important than long-term retention
- you are looking for a needle in a haystack
- the unemployment rate is historically low
- they have a track record of sourcing fantastic passive talent

Section 2: Screening

Chapter 8: Track and Qualify Applicants

Qualifying or filtering applicants effectively can save the hiring team a lot of time, and a good tracking system can aid in getting A-players. Let's assume you are now receiving resumes from whichever sources you have chosen. If you are hiring in a high unemployment market and receive over 100 resumes, then you may disqualify resumes for reasons you would not if you received less than 30 resumes. I am not saying to lower your standards in a low unemployment market, but with fewer candidates who fit the profile, you'll need to dig deeper.

Before you interview anyone in person, you should have the candidate fill out an application. Not only is it a good compliancy tool, but it is also a great filter. This will save you lots of time.

What should I look for in an application?

Any number of things can throw red flags on an application or resume.

- Employment gaps (-)
- Short history at many companies (-)
- Upward trajectory (+)
- Achievement pattern (+)
- This job is a step up (+), step down (-) or a lateral move
- Following directions: if the job posting specified "email jobs@yourcompany.com with your resume and cover letter" and you only received a resume through ZipRecruiter (not to the specified email address), you may have someone who has difficulty with details, and/or following directions (-)

The following you would typically find out from an application, but there is other very telling information that you should learn:

- Don't ask for just a salary – ask for starting and final salary (see Note 2 below)
- Ask for the manager's name (title can be helpful too)
- Ask them to rank that manager
- Ask them to guess what that manager would say about their performance
- Ask the reason for leaving and who decided to terminate the relationship (employee, company or mutual)

IMPORTANT NOTE: Inform applicant that PRIOR to an offer, you may ask to arrange an interview with the supervisor. This should draw more truthful information into the application. It may also cause underperformers to drop out, since they know that their half-truths will be discovered.

Note 2: One state, Massachusetts, passed a law forbidding asking about past salary info in the Equal Pay Law that goes into effect in 2018. Other states may follow. The intent is to compensate women on par with men in similar positions.

For an application template that uncovers these things, go to PerfectHireBlueprint.com/Resources.

Depending the website(s) you are using to source candidates, you can screen them directly in the website dashboard. Most hiring sites also send the account administrator an email for each new applicant. It is sometimes helpful to use an external tool to help filter candidates.

There are many free or low cost project planning tools online. Large companies have comprehensive Applicant Tracking Systems (ATS). These can have many features and can be expensive. For smaller companies there are fewer affordable choices. Google recently announced *Hire* that is good if you are using G Suite (Gmail, Calendar & Docs, etc.). We recommend Asana for use as an ATS because it does a good job at organizing and communicating, and it is free. Here's how we use Asana:

Using Asana

Enter qualified applicants into Asana:

- Create one "project" for each position
- Each applicant is a "task"
- Proper tagging (active, need to contact, contacted recently, leads, consider later), referral source, contact information in notes, attach resume, place in funnel, and person responsible for the next step in the process
- Record all interactions in comments (date of application, date initially contacted, date of phone screen, etc.)
- Assign due dates to make sure nobody slips through the cracks
- "Add Section" to file applicants into groups. For example, in the image below the sections are Active, Need to Ping, Pinged Recently, and Leads.

Qualify remaining applicants: use a filtering system ("sections" in Asana) known to ALL involved in the selection/interview process. This makes it easy for anyone to see where a particular candidate is along the hiring process.

- Send notes to unqualified applicants
    - How do you know they are unqualified? Refer to the skills from Job Profile.

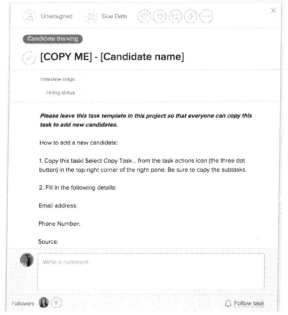

Candidate tracking

[COPY ME] - [Candidate name]

Interview stage
Hiring status

Please leave this task template in this project so that everyone can copy this task to add new candidates.

How to add a new candidate:

1. Copy this task! Select Copy Task... from the task actions icon (the three dot button) in the top-right corner of the right pane. Be sure to copy the subtasks.

2. Fill in the following details:

Email address:

Phone Number:

Source:

Move fast – great candidates likely have other companies pursuing them. If you have a great system in place for following up and moving them along the process quickly, they are more likely to stick with the process.

Have a GREAT candidate (passive or in demand)? Consider being a bit more lenient when it comes to the application process – maybe have the phone screen before the application, just so the candidates are getting something from you without investing too much time first.

A strong candidate, A-player, will have many suitors and she will have to filter jobs in some way because people need to narrow choices down to 2 or 3. Don't give her a reason to filter your company out. Your tracking system should ensure effective communication to attract A-Players.

Get More Role Specific Information

One way to qualify – or disqualify – candidates easily and quickly is to send them a follow-up email regarding their experience, habits and desires. Choose 2-5 questions that are important to the job and send a short email to all candidates you have deemed qualified by resume. Do this before asking for an application to get them engaged, since filling out a thorough application can be time consuming.

Sample email:

Subject: Your [POSITION] application - a few more questions

Hi [NAME],

Thank you for applying to the [POSITION] position at [COMPANY].

We have a few more questions for you regarding your interest in the position. Please reply to this email with your answers:

1. Why does a part time position work best for you?
2. What is your desired compensation?
3. What kind of working environment is best for you?

Thank you,
[YOUR NAME]

Your About Company line

Why ask questions in this email?

Many people will apply because it is so easy to do, even though you have said, "do not apply if..." In many of those cases, the person who is not really ready to invest time in the position will drop out by not replying to the email inquiry. If they are not engaged enough to answer, just let them go and disqualify them for this job.

Also, people will often show their true colors in a more informal communication such as a casual email. Even though it is coming from the hiring manager, it is phrased in such a way so that there are no right or wrong answers. If a candidate's answers are way off base, you are able to disqualify them earlier in the process, saving both of you time. For example, maybe you don't want a student to fill the open position, because there is the risk that they would eventually graduate and move on.

No answer from (who appears to be) a great candidate? Send a follow up email after a few days have passed. It could be that they are working many hours at their current job, or simply that life got in the way that week.

Sample email:

Subject: Re: Your [POSITION] application - a few more questions

Hi [NAME],

I haven't heard back from you – please see my email below about the [POSITION] position:

Thank you for applying to the [POSITION] position at [COMPANY].

We have a few more questions for you regarding your interest in the position. Please reply to this email with your answers:

1. Why does a part time position work best for you?
2. What is your desired compensation?
3. What kind of working environment is best for you?

Thank you,
[YOUR NAME]

Your About Company line

No answer even after you've nudged them? Either schedule a phone interview if you are very interested, or send a "closed application" email. People want what they can't have, so if you say that their window of opportunity is closing, you may get a response.

Sample email:

> Subject: Your application for [POSITION] at [COMPANY] has been closed
>
> Dear [NAME],
>
> Thank you for your interest in the [POSITION] position at [COMPANY]. Since we have not received a response from you, we are considering your application closed. Please let us know if we have overlooked your response.
>
> We wish you the best of luck in your job search.
>
> Sincerely,
>
> [NAME] at [COMPANY]
>
> Your About Company line

If you don't receive a response from this email, that's fine – you can move on. But some candidates will take this email as a wake-up call, and send you the information you requested.

You may have noticed that I recommend putting your company "about" line at the bottom of the emails. This about line should be fine-tuned to be short yet tell the great things about your company. It is another opportunity to sell your company and remind the candidate why they want to work to get the job.

If the role is very specialized, consider asking for video proof that applicant knows the job (this becomes easier daily):

Ex1: Marketing – Create a video, post it, blog on it, and email in link

Ex 2: Sales – Make a video selling the product to me. (Don't worry about video quality)

Ex 3: Show video of your expertise. If a personal trainer, show a training session; if a machinist, show your work; if a minister, send sermon, etc.

Summary & Action Items

What should I look for in an application?

- Employment gaps
- Jumping from company to company
- Short history at many companies
- Upward trajectory
- Achievement pattern
- Following directions

Qualify remaining applicants: use a filtering system known to ALL involved in the selection/interview process (we recommend Asana)

Send notes to unqualified applicants

Move fast - have a GREAT candidate? May need to be a bit more lenient

Send candidates a follow-up email regarding their experience, habits and desires.

Why ask questions in this email?

Disqualify - people will often show their true colors in a more informal communication such as a casual email.

Chapter 9: Rejecting Candidates

We've all been on the receiving end of a bad hiring process. There's nothing worse than not knowing where you stand with a company, or waiting months to hear back from a hiring manager – except never hearing anything at all!

You want to leave every candidate with a good impression of your company, in case they are desirable for a future position, or if they know someone else who is applying to the company who could be a great fit. Let everyone know their status as soon as you can, no matter where they are in the process.

Key points of communication:

- We have received your resume
- Waiting for response from questions
- Phone screen process
- Interview process
- Extend offer or reject candidate
- Post offer communication to ensure they show up day 1

Rejection – how do I do it?

If you have spoken with the person and they have come in for an interview at the company, I've found that the best, most personal way to reject a candidate is by a quick phone call by the hiring manager. That way, they can hear the tone of your voice and know that you value them and their time enough to make the call. If the candidate is a referral (from friend, employee, etc.), it is best to speak with them.

If the candidate isn't that far along in the hiring process, an email will do just fine, and this can be delivered by HR or the recruiter. Remember that negative opinions or experiences with your company can end up on Glassdoor (or another review site), so treat everyone with respect.

Sample rejection email:

> Subject: Your application for [POSITION] at [COMPANY]
>
> Hi [NAME],
>
> Thanks so much for considering the [POSITION] position at [COMPANY], and for taking the time to connect with me. After careful consideration, we regret to inform you that your experience does not match our current needs. We will keep your application on file and contact you should our needs change in the future. Best of luck in your job search.
>
> Sincerely,
> [YOUR NAME] at [COMPANY]

Summary & Action Items

Let everyone know their status as soon as you can, no matter where they are in the process.

Key points of communication:

- We have received your resume
- Waiting for response from questions
- Phone screen process
- Interview process
- Extend offer or reject candidate
- Post offer communication to ensure they show up day 1

If the candidate isn't that far along in the hiring process, an email will do just fine.

The company's perception in the market can be affected by poor rejection communication.

Chapter 10: Phone Screen

At this point you should have heard back from those you sent questions. If you've written your job description well, only those who are a good fit should have applied. If they look to be a perfect fit and you are not overwhelmed with applicants, you can skip the email screening and go to this step directly.

Within one week of receiving the resume (and email questions if applicable), schedule quick phone screens with qualified candidates. Send qualified candidates an email to set a date and time for the call. Be specific about your company and the title of the position – often candidates are applying to dozens of job listings.

Sample script for a candidate you are on the fence about, or a listing for which there are many applicants:

> "Thanks so much for your interest in the [POSITION] position at [COMPANY].
>
> Your background and work experience appears to be in line with the skill set we are looking for at [COMPANY]. I would be interested in chatting with you further regarding this job opportunity over the phone.
>
> Before we talk, please take a look at the detailed job description on our website to get a better understanding of the scope of this position.
>
> [Link to job listing]

Just to highlight a couple of points, I do want to make sure you understand the following about employment at [Company]:

[Non-negotiables/important info]

After reviewing the job description, if you are still interested in learning more about joining the [COMPANY] team, please email me with days and times you would be available to talk.

[Hours you are available]

I look forward to hearing from you soon to set up a time to talk in person.

Take Care,

[Your name]

For a great candidate, don't keep qualifying – be encouraging:

Hi [NAME],

Thank you for applying to [COMPANY]! You may be a great match for us.

I would like to schedule a time with you to discuss the [POSITION] position. Can you let me know when you have time for a quick (5-10 minutes) call in the next week or so?

Thank you,

[YOUR NAME]

Conduct Phone Interviews with Qualified Candidates

Why conduct a phone screen? Why not just bring in a candidate whose resume looks good?

We conduct phone screens to save ourselves the time and hassle of bringing someone in for an interview who may be a productivity sapping Mis-fit. You can find out a lot about a person during just a quick phone call.

The phone screen is to make sure there is a normal sounding human on the other end. Obviously it will depend on the job they're interviewing for, but if someone can't even hold a conversation and they're applying for a job that requires great interpersonal skills, it's not going to work.

There are always people who won't read the whole job ad, or gloss over the parts they don't like, in hopes that it will be negotiable (even when you say, "If this does not describe you, please don't apply"). Some people are just clicking buttons on job websites, in hopes that someone will bite.

Here is why we conduct phone interviews:

1. We once interviewed a woman for a job in which the ad clearly stated "Must be okay with large dogs" since the culture was to have dogs in the office. The woman I interviewed first asked me how big the dogs were, then she told me that she would not be okay with any size of dogs. People will say anything to get an interview - needless to say, we did not proceed with her as a candidate.
2. Someone we interviewed on the phone looked really good on paper and had great answers to the emailed questions, but couldn't carry a conversation. This particular job

posting was for an administrative position that required a lot of client facing contact and phone/conversation skills. The online communication was good, but the applicant would not have been successful in the position. (But task-based people can be excellent writers.)

3. We posted an opening for a part-time job on ZipRecruiter and Indeed. The job was listed in the "Part-time" category on both websites. The part-time hours were referenced in the job posting in 3 places: once at the top, once in the middle (with more detail on specific hours), and once at the end. One of the questions in the follow-up email asked, "Why does a part-time position work for you?" The woman we were phone screening had replied via email with her answer about wanting a part-time position. When we got her on the phone, she was completely unaware that the position was part time, even though there were many barriers in place to prevent a situation like this.

Interviewing someone who is clearly unqualified for the position is a huge waste of time and resources for both the employer and the job seeker. It's best to try to only let qualified applicants in the door, and the phone screen is a quick, effective method! If you bring a Mis-fit in for an interview, it does not help company morale because your A-Player interviewers see that you either wasted their time, or the candidate will lower the talent caliber of the company.

How to phone screen

This phone screen should be more than just a quick call to ensure the candidate can string a few words together. "Building rapport" starts with this phone call, and it should also be the first filter to determine if the hiring manger and others should invest their time interviewing the candidate. It is also a time when a great candidate starts deciding if your company is worth their time, or if they can picture themselves working at the company.

What are you trying to accomplish in a phone screen?

- Verbal ability, and motivation (motivation for applying and general self-motivation)
- Getting a feel for the applicant that is not apparent via text – sometimes I can discount someone right off the bat (e.g., if they are notably unenergetic for a position that requires high energy), and sometimes I am surprised since the way they behave via text is opposite of their behavior on the phone
- Gauging their excitement about the company/position
- Giving them more details about the position (remember, all interactions are a two-way street— you are being qualified by the applicant as well)

How long is the phone screen?

- For an individual contributor position, typically 5-10 minutes, though some will go shorter/longer based on applicant's personality and the position
- For a leadership/manager position, it takes longer to ask about management style to determine cultural fit

Sample intro script:

"Hi [NAME], this is [YOUR NAME] calling from [COMPANY]. Thanks for taking the time to connect with me today. I was hoping you could answer a few questions for me about your background and experience with [JOB OPENING].

What questions do you ask?

    a. Can you tell me a bit about your background as [POSITION]?

    b. What are you doing currently?

    c. Reason for leaving previous position?

    d. Why are you looking for a new opportunity?

    e. Why do you think you would be a good fit for this position?/How could you be successful in this role?

    f. What interests you most about this position?

    g. Could you clarify [SOMETHING ON RESUME]?

    h. How would you characterize your management style?

    i. Do you have any questions for me?

    j. What kind of company cultures have you work in? What did you think of them?

    k. What is your ideal work environment?

    l. Have your roles and responsibilities ever changed unexpectedly?

    m. Have you had a manager who gives blunt feedback?

    n. What's the greatest mistake you ever made?

Add notes to the candidate's record in your tracking tool. Once the first phone screen determines if the candidate is suitable for the position, the candidate is tagged in the database as "Passed phone interview" or "Did not pass phone interview." Add notes from your call for more detail.

Assign applicants who pass this screen to next interviewer: If the next interviewer is a different person, the candidate must be notified. Schedule the interview with the candidate over email, and let her know to look for the email from the next interviewer. Debrief phone screen details with second interviewer.

PHB Tip: Video conferencing can be an effective tool for screening for customer facing jobs. Skype or Zoom are affordable and easy to use. Video can help identify things such as nervous tics or eye contact issues before bringing the person in for an interview. This can also be a cost effective measure if the candidate needs to fly in for the interview.

Summary & Action Items

Within one week of receiving the resume, schedule quick phone screens with qualified candidates.

Save the time and hassle of bringing someone in for an interview who is not a good fit.

What are you trying to accomplish in a phone screen?

- Verbal ability, and motivation
- Getting a feel for the applicant that is not apparent via text
- Gauging their excitement about the company/position
- Giving them more details about the position

Add notes to the candidate's record in your tracking tool

Assign applicants to next interviewer

Chapter 11: Have a Pre-Interview Meet-up

Some hiring managers think that the in-person interview is supposed to be stressful, so that you can better gauge how the candidate may perform under stress at work. I have three answers to that:

1. **There shouldn't be that much stress at work.**
2. **You will not get a true read on the candidate's natural behavior at work.**
3. **The candidate will not want to work for your company.**

(Note: Positions that require the employee to often walk in to unfamiliar and potentially emotionally charged environments can/should skip this step because it is part of the job. This step is best for office-based and home-based jobs.)

The goal of the interviewing process is to create a composite of how the candidate will perform in the job as described. But, the interview is not a natural setting- it is already stressful. The interviewee is trying to be who she thinks you want her to be, and the interviewer is "judging." Often, minds are made up in the first 60-90 seconds. This "interrogation" is not a comfortable situation for any interaction, whether it is a teenager coming home after curfew, or a candidate interviewing for a job.

To have a better chance of seeing how someone will really behave if hired, **I recommend that the hiring manager have a face-to-face meeting for about 30 minutes before the formal interview.** One great place to have this is at a coffee shop, and have it occur a day or two before the interview. This is especially important for a job that tends to draw introverts, or people with lower social skills. This is typical of those with analytical

backgrounds, for instance. (I highly recommend a Job
Profile/Benchmark to identify these traits.)

**There are many good reasons to have a pre-interview
meeting:**

- More casual - less stilted
- Less stressful for the candidate
- Prescreen for any anomalies – strange behavior or
  appearance
- Isolate strange behavior early – don't bring it into the
  office
- More realistic view of behavior – not under the spotlight
- Better in-office interview – fewer unknowns means more
  comfort
- Saves time and resources – don't schedule an interview day
  with a known Mis-fit
- The candidate will be more comfortable at the interview

The ideal environment is a coffee shop for several reasons:

- Short amount of time – much less than with a meal
- Neutral ground – no one has home field advantage
- In public – likely won't make a scene, safer for strangers to
  meet
- Comfort of knowing what to expect of the interview
  environment – likely been to one before
- Low cost – any budget can afford a coffee meeting
- Daily routine – may already be going there in the AM
- Fits the candidate's schedule – won't have to take time off
  from current job.
  (Important: tell the candidate to dress as he would typically –
  and "don't judge the book by its cover/outfit")

Remember, this is not a formal interview. It is a casual
conversation to get to know the candidate. Don't bring a prepared
list of questions or give a test. Keep it light and topical.

How can I keep the conversation casual?

Start with:

> How are you? Can I get you a coffee? (Another drink if not coffee?) Need a small bite to eat? I am getting _____.
> Did you run into any traffic on your way here? The construction/road conditions are... When do you need to leave? What do you think of this weather?

Continue with: Just let the conversation go – don't steer it. See where the candidate takes it.

End with:

> Just wanted to get to know you a little bit. We have a process to make sure we hire only very good people. You'll hear from _____ about the next step. We have some very good candidates, so it may not be immediate.
>
> If good candidate: Are there any times or days we should avoid? Please be patient if you can. I believe you will find the result to be worth the effort. We will go as fast as we can. Please call me if you have any concerns. (Give your personal business card to the best candidates)

Disclaimer: While it may be casual, it is still technically an interview. Don't cross the line by talking about personal, non-job related topics that may make the candidate less desirable in your mind (for example: relationships, children, extra-curriculars, military activity, criminal record, age, religion, etc.). This can be easy to fall into since it is a casual conversation. If the candidate brings up one of the "out of bounds" topics, make a mental note of it and move on. Don't keep digging.

Positions where I don't recommend this meeting:

I don't think it is as good of an idea to have a pre-interview meeting for a position such as an outside salesperson or senior execute who needs to make a great first impression and adapt to any in-person situation. It will be common for those people to be in unknown situations, and it is more than fair to see how they would react to the unknowns.

If you still feel good about the candidate after this pre-interview meet-up, move them to the next step in the process: the interview at the company. Asana notifies the hiring manager that the candidate is in the queue and next steps are the responsibility of the manager.

1. **Assign applicant to next interviewer for face-to-face interview at the company**
   a. Add notes to contact record
   b. Next interviewer schedules interview
2. **Contact applicant to schedule interview** – Depends on department

* * *

PHB TIP: If you have multiple candidates to interview, **interview the weakest first.** Here's why:

1. It allows you to work out the kinks in your interview process on a less critical candidate.
2. You will incorporate lessons learned into the more important interviews.
3. If you interview the best first, you may lose the person before you get around to making an offer. This will help you schedule the candidates closer together and take action more quickly.

Summary & Action Items

A face-to-face meeting before the formal interview is
recommended to have a better chance of seeing how someone will
really behave if hired.

There are many good reasons to have a pre-interview meeting:

- More casual - less stilted
- Less stressful for the candidate
- Prescreen for any anomalies
- Isolate strange behavior early
- More realistic view of behavior
- Better in-office interview
- Saves time and resources
- The candidate will be more comfortable at the interview

Assign applicant to next interviewer for face-to-face interview at
the company

Add notes to contact record

Next interviewer schedules interview

Contact applicant to schedule interview

Chapter 12: First Interview

The in-person interview continues the process by having management and key employees ask specific questions to get a gut feel of the candidate and decide if she should be moved to the next step in the process. The interview day is also when the candidate decides if she can work for your company and the hiring manager, so you need to sell the company as well as interview the candidate.

Many companies don't understand the full importance of the on-site interview. If CEOs actually considered what is at stake, I believe many would have a better plan for the candidate's visit.

An interview should:

- **Sell** the value of the company
- **Qualify** the candidate
- **Communicate** the culture of the company
- **Show** the caliber of people the candidate will work with
- **Convey** a typical day of working at the company
- **Identify** if the candidate is a good fit for the company and the position.

Does your company have a plan for who asks which interview questions? Is it a well-choreographed endeavor? If it isn't, your company may not only be missing a great opportunity, but it may also be missing out on hiring the best candidates for the company.

* * *

To hire the best workers, the in-person or on-site interview should be 70% interview and 30% selling.

* * *

Great candidates, A-players, will not be there to just get the job. **A-players want to work with other A-players at a great company.** You will not attract A-players with B-players, so put your best and brightest on the interview team.

Selling the company is not a sales pitch, but should be done by your A-players talking about why they work there – what keeps your top talent motivated? Your A-players should either be asking behavioral interviewing questions, answering questions, or injecting why they work there. Otherwise, the candidate should be talking.

Choreographing the on-site visit is very important, and the post-interview team debrief is also vital. The team needs to hear about the responses to key questions from the people who asked the questions.

PHB TIP: Inform the candidate that you will be asking for references (prior managers preferred) and will check those references. This candidate should "stretch the truth" about his experience to a lesser extent if the exaggeration may be detected in a reference check.

Day of interview checklist

- ☑ Stay objective – fight against falling victim to first impressions.
- ☑ The manager should start by setting the stage:
    - ○ Get the candidate excited about the opportunity.
    - ○ Describe what success looks like at the company.
    - ○ Explain what to expect from interview process.
    - ○ It is a mistake to start with someone other than the hiring manager, unless he is too inexperienced.
- ☑ Administer the job competency test. Some examples are:

- o Personal trainers should put the interviewer through a typical training session.
- o A chef should cook his signature dish.
- o An analyst could develop a spreadsheet from a specification.
- o An engineer or programmer should understand the theory behind the technology, design something related, or correct a flaw.
- ☑ A tour of the company typically makes sense. It should be done by an employee who has done a tour previously to show the highlights and not get bogged down in the details.
- ☑ Each interviewer has an assignment:
  - o Multiple stakeholders – 30 minutes each (hiring manager decides on interviewers)
  - o Each interviewer asks different questions
    - ▪ Refer to the Multi-respondent Job Report from the Benchmarking process for interview questions that identify the perfect hire.
  - o These questions are behavioral – what happened in the past will likely happen again.
  - o Ask for specific examples, don't stay at 10 thousand feet. Get specifics on results:
    - ▪ Ex. When you said that $200k was sold, how much did you personally do?
    - ▪ Ex. What role did you personally play in the success of that project?
    - ▪ Probe – Why, When, How, What?
    - ▪ Get details – size, scope, complexity, effort, team issues, dates, etc.
  - o Looking for Action and Execution – not generalities and what the "group" accomplished.
  - o Find out what the environment was like, whether it worked for her, and determine how it is similar to or differs from your environment.

- o Did the person act as a leader of others (even informally)?
- o What motivates the person to do their best?

☑ QUESTIONS MUST PERTAIN TO THE JOB, NOT ONE'S PERSONAL LIFE OUTSIDE OF WORK.
- o If the person is not hired, any conversation regarding what is done on personal time could be scrutinized.
- o For example, you can't ask what they do for fun after work, but you can ask if they achieve a healthy work/life balance.

☑ Stay away from the following topics. Most of these subjects relate directly to federal and state employment laws. In an interview, or on an employment application, do not ask questions about...
- o Age: Be careful using the words "over qualified" with older candidates.
- o Arrest record (this is different from convictions - in most states, it is permissible to ask if the candidate has ever been convicted of a crime).
- o Race or ethnicity
- o Citizenship (though it is permissible to ask "Will you be able to provide proof of eligibility to work in the U.S. if hired?")
- o Ancestry, birthplace or native language (though it is permissible to ask about their ability to speak English or a foreign language if required for the job)
- o Religion, customs or holidays
- o Height and weight: if it does not affect their ability to perform the job, don't ask.
- o Relatives: Only those relatives employed by the organization are permitted.

- o Living arrangements (including rent or own): Asking for their address for future contact is acceptable.
- o Credit history or financial situation: In some cases, credit history may be considered job-related, but be cautious.
- o Education or training, if not required for the job.
- o Sex or gender. Avoid any language or behavior that the candidate may find inappropriate.
- o Pregnancy or medical history: Attendance history is mostly ok. Don't refer to disability or illness.
- o Family or marital status or child-care: (OK to ask if the candidate can work the required hours).
- o Membership in a non-professional organization if not related to the job.
- o Physical or mental disabilities: Can ask whether the candidate can perform the essential job duties.
- ☑ As a rule of thumb, don't ask non-job-related questions. Check your local laws to be sure. See PerfectHireBlueprint.com/Resources for more about legal issues in hiring.

PHB Tip: Have two interviewers in the room with the candidate at the same time. This allows one to ask a question and write the answer, while the next interviewer asks his next question. It saves time, and is more accurate. If done in a welcoming way, it can put the candidate at ease more than a one-on-one.

- ☑ Before leaving, the candidate should take a TriMetrix Assessment if hiring manager deems the candidate may be qualified.
  - o I recommend the candidate take the Assessment before leaving the company on the day of the interview. Not only does it move the process along

faster, but she is guaranteed to complete it if she is on site still.

- o Alternatively, if the candidate did not budget enough time to do the Assessment well, allow them to take it later. This is better than rushing the Assessment, which typically takes 30-45 minutes.

☑ A post-interview roundtable meeting is held with all interviewers to debrief to the manager.

☑ The manager is responsible for the hire, so it is the manager's call how the decision to hire is made:

- o Can be solely by the manager, if authority is obtained.
- o Can be a majority of the interviewers if the manager prefers.
- o Can be the call of the manager and his supervisor(s) if unsure.

Effective Interview Questions

What was the most interesting interview question you've ever been asked? Why did you find it interesting? Was it effective at identifying you as a good candidate? What do you think was the purpose of the question?

Here are Glassdoor's Top 10 Oddball Interview Questions for 2015, and the companies that asked them:

1. "What would you do if you were the one survivor in a plane crash?" - Airbnb
2. "What's your favorite 90s jam?" – Squarespace
3. "If you woke up and had 2,000 unread emails and could only answer 300 of them, how would you choose which ones to answer?" – Dropbox
4. Who would win in a fight between Spiderman and Batman?" – Stanford University

5. "If you had a machine that produced $100 for life, what would you be willing to pay for it today?" – Aksia
6. "What did you have for breakfast?" – Banana Republic
7. "Describe the color yellow to somebody who's blind." – Spirit Airlines
8. "If you were asked to unload a 747 full of jelly beans, what would you do?" – Bose
9. "How many people flew out of Chicago last year?" – Redbox
10. "What's your favorite Disney Princess?" – Cold Stone Creamery

Hopefully there was a reason these questions were asked. Some could be icebreakers or give an indication of company culture. Others determine how people think or approach a problem. Every question should have a purpose.

Other great interview questions:

1. Tell me a time when something didn't go right.
    a. Don't talk - just listen. (if anything, say, "Tell me more")
    b. Bad responses:
        i. If blames others or is bitter – not good for your culture
        ii. If not including himself – not accountable
    c. Good responses:
        i. Regret/guilt for not performing better
        ii. Lesson learned
        iii. Takes ownership
2. What accomplishment from your last job brought you the most pride?
    a. Ask why they chose that situation
    b. Bad responses:
        i. What the group accomplished

- You are looking for what the person can do. If the answer is a result done with a team, dig deeper to ask what he actually did
    - ii. Appears to be a typical run-of-the-mill issue
    - iii. Struggles to find one
        - A-players know when they've done well
    - c. Good responses:
        - i. Had a very difficult issue, and resolved it with determination and resiliency.
        - ii. Manager asked her specifically because she was uniquely qualified. She exceeded expectations.
        - iii. Was asked to step up and lead. Desired outcome was achieved (even if with difficulty).
3. Why did you leave your last company? What factors entered into that decision?
    - a. Remind them that you want them to set up a reference check for you with that company.
        - i. This tactic not only gets a more truthful answer, but also increases the odds of a good reference check.
    - b. Bad responses:
        - i. Blaming others: Bad manager, wasn't treated fairly, didn't respect me (these issues don't go away by changing jobs).
        - ii. Was fired.
        - iii. Was laid off (if the entire group was not let go).
            - Indicates not an A-player.
    - c. Good responses:
        - i. I wanted to do X for my own career growth, but there wasn't an opportunity to do that at that company. I got it at my next job.

    ii.   I liked the company, but the new career opportunity was just too good pass up.

   iii.   Needed to relocate for family reasons.

   iv.   I moved to take a dream job.

- Most people have a company in mind. Many would relocate to work at Google, Tesla, Disney or Apple among others.

What is accomplished by asking questions such as these? Does it give insight into the prospective employee? Does it put a company in the right light in the candidate's eyes?

One the oddest interview questions I've heard is, **"What's the first thing you know?"** It was used multiple times in the early 90s by a Regional Manager in Dallas. This question stumped many people. It can be the start of a "stress interview" or it can be an icebreaker, depending on how long the interviewer allows the candidate to struggle.

A great interview question might be, **"What did you do to prepare for this interview today?"** This uncovers how the candidate prepares for something important (or if she thinks the opportunity is important).

This should be asked by only one interviewer. **ALL** questions should be asked by only one interviewer. This is not only more efficient, but also more effective. Savvy candidates will learn from the first time a question is asked. The second time, she may answer it the way she thinks the company wants it answered, and this will make her look like a better candidate.

The other reason for consistent questioning is that it is easier for the team to compare candidates. For more information on great interview questions, go to PerfectHireBlueprint.com/Resources.

(By the way, there is only one correct answer for "What's the first thing you know?", and I can almost guarantee that no Millennial would get it. Baby boomers are more likely to get it, and even then, it's likely a small number. The answer is..."Ol' Jed's a millionaire." If you still don't get it, play the Beverly Hillbillies theme song in your head. When the interviewer gave the answer, the candidate typically relaxed a bit.)

* * *

ALL questions should be asked by only one interviewer. This is not only more efficient, but also more effective.

* * *

After the interview, each interviewer should fill out a Candidate Interview Evaluation Form. These results will be compared to the Assessment for further team calibration. Visit PerfectHireBlueprint.com/Resources to download the form.

Company Culture

The culture of your company plays a large part in hiring A-players. Just because someone is an A-player elsewhere does not mean that he will be an A-player at your company doing basically the same job. The company values shape the culture, even if the values are not explicitly stated.

For example, one company could have a pacesetting, aggressive growth culture, and another could have a more laid-back culture of fun and happiness. A hard driving A-player may not fit in at the latter company.

It is important to uncover what motivates the candidate during the interview. Your unique culture could be motivating or demotivating. If there is no culture match, a great candidate can become a nightmare employee.

* * *

Look for good role models – yours might be a good parent or good friend. Hire people who might even be a better person than you are.

* * *

Right now you're probably worried that you don't have a stated culture, or that you can't articulate it. DON'T WORRY, we've got you covered. The Job Profile/Benchmark uncovers the values/motivators of the company, as contributed by those who contributed the Job Assessments.

Additionally, it will report what motivators (aka Driving Forces) are important for someone doing the job in question. Sometimes a job can require different values.

A Sales position is a good example of how a company and a job could ideally have different values. In most cases, salespeople need to be motivated by money – almost "coin operated" if you will. A successful salesperson typically sells the product or service to a type of customer that will maximize his pay.

This may not be as predictable as you would think. Will the salesperson look for one big sale at a big prospect (the home run) or go after lots of smaller sales (single hits)?

Many times the territory dictates the tactics. This is typically true no matter the values of the company. The company may have a culture that is as famous as Google ("Googliness" is demonstrated in the movie The Internship), but the salespeople could be as aggressive as a Wall Street boiler room (portrayed in the movie The Wolf of Wall Street).

It is important that the person you hire fits the values and motivators of the role she hopes to fill. A mismatch will likely become painful while the person is employed, and will lead to another candidate search within a year.

Hiring for FIT – Value match

When companies are looking to hire employees who "fit" their company, many times they look for commonality. What they are actually looking for (or should be looking for) is common values, but in most cases the interviewer is not aware of that. Yes, they look for experience, skills, and the like, but common values are the most important thing for long term employment, according to many sources.

Values are WHY people behave the way they do.

In his book *Navigating the Growth Curve*, James Fischer states, "Creating a homogeneous group is more important in a Stage 1 company (1 to 10 employees) than putting together a highly competent group." Early on, the company needs to have a similar "why" in order to get to the next, more stable stage.

One of the best books that I've read on employee retention is *Love 'em or Lose 'em* by Beverly Kaye and Sharon Jordan-Evans. The authors say, "By 'right fit' we mean...The right person's core values are consistent with the values of the organization."

The problem I've seen most often is that most small and medium sized businesses have not stated the company's core values. Like personal values, company values tell people WHY the company does what it does. They may say that everyone knows what they are, or that we will know if a candidate's values are a match, but I have not found that to consistently improve hiring success. Candidates, particularly Millennials, want to know why the company does what it does.

First, create your company values if you don't currently have them clearly stated. You can try to do it yourself or hire a company like mine, mPower Advisors, to help you. One of the better books on mission, vision and values in my opinion is *Full Steam Ahead!* by Ken Blanchard and Jesse Lyn Stoner. The book states in part that values:

- "...answer the questions 'What do I want to live by?' and 'How'?
- need to be few in number and rank ordered in importance.
- need to be clearly described so you know exactly the behaviors that demonstrate that the value is being lived.
- need to be consistently acted on, or they are only 'good intentions.'"

While anyone can do an internet search for typical company values, each business will have its own values that are unique to the organization. Just because Southwest Airlines and Zappos are known for having great values and culture does not mean that your company should adopt their values.

For a list of values that companies may choose as important, visit PerfectHireBlueprint.com/Resources.

When a company goes through this exercise, it is important to get broad buy-in from the employees.

Then, assuming that you do have company values, the second difficulty is determining if the prospective employee has the same values as your company.

It is true that knowledge of an individual's values helps to tell us WHY they do things. Knowing a candidate's experiences, education and training will help to know WHAT they can do. Behavioral Assessments help to tell us HOW a person behaves and performs in the work environment.

The values or personal motivators do not change significantly without a life changing event. Yes, I've seen people become more financially driven in time (for instance, where income is limited), but once the balance is restored, the focus on money goes back to where it was before, a short term blip. But if someone has personally had a serious health concern, some of the things he thought were important become less so as the thought of longevity seems less likely.

One way to determine what a person values is to look to researchers. Eduard Spranger, a German researcher, authored *Types of Men*, which was translated into English in 1928. The information in this book still holds true today.

The six basic interests or values (a way of valuing life) are Theoretical, Utilitarian/Economic, Aesthetic, Social/Altruistic, Individualistic/Political and Traditional/Regulatory. The six are defined as:

- Traditional/Regulatory - Rewards those who value traditions inherent in social structure, rules, regulations and principles.
- Aesthetic - Rewards those who value balance in their lives, creative self-expression, beauty and nature.
- Individualistic/Political - Rewards those who value personal recognition, freedom, and control over their own destiny and others.

- Theoretical - Rewards those who value knowledge for knowledge's sake, continuing education and intellectual growth.
- Social/Altruistic - Rewards those who value opportunities to be of service to others and contribute to the progress and well-being of society.
- Utilitarian/Economic - Rewards those who value practical accomplishments, results and rewards for their investments of time, resources and energy.

The descriptions are for one who is high in that value and they tell "why you do what you do." They are sometimes called the **hidden motivators** because they are not always readily observed. And the top 2 values/motivators drive behavior more than the bottom 4. What has been researched further in recent years is that the **HIGHER 2 of the 6 may not be the TOP 2 of the 6**.

Recent research has determined that the top 2 are the two that are the FARTHEST from the norm, or average. So someone with a very LOW rating in a motivator/value might be driven more by that low rating any other high rating. This revelation has changed the landscape very recently.

The late Bill Bonstetter of TTI Success Insights took this research to new heights and he put labels to the low and high of each for the previously known motivators. They are:

	High		Low
Theoretical:	Intellectual	<--------->	Instinctive
Utilitarian:	Resourceful	<--------->	Selfless
Aesthetic:	Harmonious	<--------->	Objective
Social:	Altruistic	<--------->	Intentional
Individualistic:	Commanding	<--------->	Collaborative
Traditional:	Structured	<--------->	Receptive

So, for example, a high Theoretical is now an Intellectual, and a low Theoretical is now Instinctive.

Would your company use terms like collaborative, structured/systematic, harmonious, selfless or objective to describe its values or culture? If so, it would be helpful to have an Assessment that could determine whether a candidate has these motivators. The outcome of the Assessment would determine if the job is a good fit for her for the long term. This is valuable information for a company to know about its employees since values initiate or drive our behavioral style.

What if your company does not have stated values?

No problem. In an earlier chapter we reviewed the Benchmark Assessment. This Assessment not only determines the values of the company from the chosen stakeholders who take the Assessment for the Benchmark, but also the values/motivators needed for the job.

While this is not a complete list of company values, it is a good start. When the Gap Report highlights the differences between the candidate's values (from the Assessment) and the company's values (from the Benchmark), pay attention. The smaller the gaps, the better the candidate will fit your company.

The company culture and the candidate's values need to go hand in hand. If there is not a match, the candidate will not likely be a long term employee.

Summary & Action Items

Management and key employees ask specific questions to get a gut feel of the candidate and decide if she should be moved to the next step in the process.

An interview should:

- Sell the value of the company
- Qualify the candidate
- Communicate the culture of the company
- Show the caliber of people the candidate will work with
- Convey a typical day of working at the company
- Identify if the candidate is a good fit for the company and the position.

The in-person or on-site interview should be 70% interview and 30% selling.

Day of interview checklist:

- Stay objective
- The manager should start by setting the stage
- A tour of the company typically makes sense.
- Each interviewer has an assignment
- QUESTIONS MUST PERTAIN TO THE JOB, NOT ONE'S PERSONAL LIFE OUTSIDE OF WORK.

- Before leaving, the candidate may take a TriMetrix Assessment if hiring manager deems the candidate may be qualified.
- A post-interview roundtable meeting is held with all interviewers to debrief to the manager.
- The manager is responsible for the hire, so it is the manager's call how the decision to hire is made

Company Culture and Hiring for FIT

First, create your company values if you don't currently have them clearly stated.

- "...answer the questions 'What do I want to live by?' and 'How'?
- They need to be few in number and rank ordered in importance.
- They need to be clearly described so you know exactly the behaviors that demonstrate that the value is being lived.
- They need to be consistently acted on, or they are only 'good intentions.'"

* * *

There are fewer candidates applying for each job, and there are fewer good candidates who are actively looking. The best candidates will have more opportunities than just your company.

* * *

Chapter 13: Talent Assessment & Gap Analysis

Once the candidate has passed the in-person interview, I recommend they take a Multi-Measure Assessment. The results of the Assessment are compared to the Benchmark developed at the start of the process. A Gap Report is generated to show the differences (gaps) between the Benchmark (ideal candidate) and the actual candidate.

If the Gap Report dashboard shows red or yellow flags in certain areas, get clarification from the candidate. Though it's hard sometimes to discount someone who seems like a great fit based on Assessment results, the likelihood of him succeeding in the position is low.

If the Assessment is way off of the Benchmark, you should not proceed with caution, but should STOP and take a critical look. They can say and do all the right things, but if the Gap Report shows too many discrepancies, you should look for agreement in other data points uncovered in the interview, and then let the candidate go. He will not be the right fit for the company or position.

If the Gap Report dashboard does not show red flags (an example of a good Gap Report is below), schedule a second interview with the candidate.

Job Competencies Hierarchy	Zone Range	Person	
1. Customer Focus	8.4 — 10.0	8.0	◻
2. Diplomacy & Tact	8.3 — 10.0	6.0	◻
3. Empathy	6.2 — 10.0	7.3	■
4. Resiliency	8.3 — 10.0	7.1	▨
5. Flexibility	7.6 — 8.8	8.3	■
6. Interpersonal Skills	6.8 — 9.9	8.0	■
7. Personal Accountability	8.1 — 10.0	7.7	▦

Job Rewards/Culture Hierarchy	Zone Range	Person	
1. Traditional/Regulatory	6.8 — 10.0	3.2	▨
2. Aesthetic	4.3 — 6.1	3.3	◻
3. Social	2.3 — 4.2	5.2	◻

Job Behavioral Hierarchy	Zone Range	Person	
1. Following Policy	8.0 — 10.0	7.5	▦
2. Consistent	6.1 — 8.2	8.0	■
3. People-Oriented	6.5 — 8.0	7.0	■

■ Exact match   ▨ Fair compatibility
▦ Good compatibility   ▧ Poor compatibility   ◻ Over-focused

The 3 areas that are used for the Benchmark will find you someone who will not only fit the job, but perform it very well, if the skills and knowledge are in place. One thing that you won't know is whether the person is performing at the high end of his capability or if there is still much more potential that has yet to be tapped.

Each viable candidate will be given a talent Assessment. There is a tradeoff between time and money as to the definition of "viable."

Some companies will assess every candidate to winnow down the number of people to take to the next step. Other companies use less rigorous or non-standard techniques to filter the candidates.

Many factors determine if the candidate is the right fit: the cover letter, resume, interviews, references and the online Individual Assessment. The Assessment is objective, so it cuts through the nervousness – or charisma – that the candidate displays that may affect the interviewer's perception. The Assessment also compensates for the unconscious bias of the interviewer, as discussed in the introduction.

Without the Assessment, more time is needed for in-depth reviewing of the resume, cover letter and any other information provided or garnered in the interviews and through research.

The Assessment report is like a user manual for an employee; you'll know what not to do and how to interact to benefit both the employee and the company. The stereotype says that people don't read manuals. Reading the Assessment report will likely be the difference between an OK hire and a stellar, long-term employee and key contributor.

See a sample report at PerfectHireBlueprint.com/Resources.

Summary & Action Items

Once the candidate has passed the in-person interview, she should take a Multi-Measure Assessment. A Gap Report shows the differences between the Benchmark and the actual candidate.

If the Gap Report does not show red flags, schedule a second interview.

Chapter 14: Second Interview

The second interview needs to primarily gather more data on the areas of concern from the first interview and the Assessment. The hiring manager should be the primary interviewer.

This is also the best time to bring in someone above the hiring manager to both confirm that the hire is the right person, and to make the interviewee feel important by gaining access to the higher level person.

Remember, the company still needs to get the candidate excited about working there. You may now have a great candidate, so now it is time to get the hire ready to accept.

Maybe this interview is a 2-by-1, where the hiring manager, subject matter expert (SME), and the candidate have a conversation. This can be especially helpful if the SME does not have the best social skills (picture Sheldon from The Big Bang Theory).

The manager can clarify (or translate) what the SME says to the candidate, IF the candidate doesn't seem to understand – let the peer talk uninterrupted if possible. Have the person who is not asking the question take good notes. This allows the one who asked the questions to keep eye contact.

This is also a great time to dive deep into the resume, asking specifics about past managers. Listen closely for negative talk about previous managers. The candidate should talk about what was learned, what went well and what didn't. But, if in talking about reasons for leaving the manager is thrown under the bus, this is something that should be explored further.

If it appears that EVERY manager was below par or had an issue with the candidate, it is likely that the issue is not with the past managers. If you hire this candidate, you may be the next in a long line of disappointed managers.

Use the questions provided by the Job Report from the Benchmarking process that pertain to the areas of concern from the Assessment. Based on the answers to the questions, discern if the gaps from the report can be sufficiently bridged.

This process of using the provided questions will be more objective than the first interview. This will help reduce any known or unknown biases, and bring to light any blind spots that were not seen in the first interviews.

Also remember to continue to make a great impression and highlight why the company and the role could be great for the right person. The goal is for the candidate to accept a reasonable offer if you make one, so the candidate has to want to work at the company.

Assuming everything went well, this is a great time to discuss the candidate's references. Stress that your rigorous hiring methods do not let weak candidates become employees. To ensure that what is on the resume is the truth, reference checks are taken seriously – this is important to A-players.

PHB Tip: A best practice is to ask the candidate to call her references to let them know to expect a call, and to be candid on that call. One more level of candidate commitment is to have her schedule the reference calls. This can save a lot of phone tag on the reference checker's part.

Making an offer at the end of the second interview, while done by some, is not recommended. Even if there were only a few areas from the Gap Report in which to dig deeper, the resume deep dive did not uncover any surprises, and the hiring manager is prepared to make an offer the same day, the reference checks (and potentially a background check) need to be executed.

That isn't to say that you can't discuss a potential offer (not a contingent offer). This can be very helpful if you have a good candidate who already has an offer from another company, or who you expect might get another offer. Moving quickly but thoroughly is a sign of a good company for which to work.

You may have heard the saying, "a trial lawyer should never ask a question to which she doesn't already know the answer." This assures they maintain control and avoid being blindsided or surprised. I think this applies to making an offer. To understand what would be accepted, this is a great time to ask if the person has any offers or expects any offers before you can complete the reference checks. If you are going to make the effort to present an offer, you want to be sure the offer will be accepted.

Then ask for salary requirements, or the compensation (salary and benefits) that would be acceptable to the candidate. That answer could tell you a lot.

If the question is answered, that is good information to take back to the roundtable (next chapter). More likely than not, you will not get a definitive answer, and you may need to dig deeper. If your candidate has another offer, ask if she is willing to share the numbers.

This can also be a time when you find out if the candidate is really serious about working for your company, or if she is just trying to get an offer (either to raise her salary at her current job, or to get another company to offer more). This interaction can sometimes feel uncomfortable, but I believe it is important to better comprehend where you stand before the control shifts to the candidate.

If you have sold the candidate on the job, you may get an answer that she is excited to get an offer, and that a competitive offer would land the candidate. Hesitation could mean that more selling is necessary.

If the hiring manager is not adept at this, Emotional Intelligence training is recommended.

Reference Checks

This is an area where many managers fall short. They either don't check references thoroughly enough, or don't check at all. The candidate should give at least 3 references, and the best are former managers, though it is understandable if the current manager is not provided.

If you can't get the current manager, try to contact someone who has left the company who was at a higher level than the candidate, who may know about her performance.

See it as a red flag if former managers are not provided by the candidate. You need to speak with the person who approved the paycheck. That person will know if the person was worth what he was paid.

Again, asking the candidate to contact her references, and having those references reach out to the person doing the hiring, will make this process easier and show the commitment of the candidate. Ideally, the candidate will schedule a time when the call will take place. This eliminates the frustrating task of phone tag with references. This is in the candidate's best interest because it reduces the time to receive an offer. I admit that this request may not be "normal" or expected by the candidate, but if she is excited about the job, she will arrange this for you. (A word of caution: some meek personalities may cringe at the thought. If it is too uncomfortable, you could lose the candidate, so don't push too hard on these types of people.)

I know some larger companies have a person in HR do the reference checks, but I disagree. Reference checking should not simply be a formality. The hiring manager needs to make the best decision possible, thus more firsthand information is important.

The manager will live with the consequences of hiring a Mis-fit, so she should ask the questions of a peer manager of the other company. Manager-to-manager and peer-to-peer conversations yield the best information.

There are the questions you should always ask, and there are the questions to be asked in areas of concern that have not been resolved in the interviews.

Start the conversation with:

- "I'm sure you want Joe to succeed, so I just want to make sure I really understand him."

This will give the manager a chance to open up.

Here are some good questions to ask:

- In what capacity did you work with Joe?
- What were his biggest strengths or value to the group?
- Would you say that Joe was in the top 25% in job performance as compared to his peers?
- If you were managing Joe today, what area(s) would you think he could improve most?

- In the interview, Joe told me the story about _____. Can you tell me what happened from your perspective?
- Joe seems to be (character trait). Do I have a correct impression of this?

In reference checks, it is important what is said, but it is also very important what is not said. The candidate gave you the references, so they should be stellar. If you are expecting to hear very positive comments, neutral responses or lack of comment would be a sign that you should not ignore.

Also listen for the tone of voice. If there is not excitement in the conversation, you should try to determine why.

Word of caution: I know at this point in the process you want this to be over. You've gone through the many steps to this point, and you've gotten your team to agree on a candidate. It is human nature to overlook a few issues. Just remind yourself that a finding out a significant issue will save you 10x the aggravation if you hire a Mis-fit.

There have been many cases where a candidate was not hired due to a poor reference, and the company that gave the less than stellar reference could be sued. A successful lawsuit would only be for defamation of character – knowingly giving false information. People don't win cases when the facts were correct, or one's opinion was given.

If the candidate gave permission to check the reference, the former employer is on even safer ground. For more articles on this topic (legality of reference checks, and a primer on defamation), visit PerfectHireBlueprint.com/Resources.

As a precaution, many HR departments of larger companies ask that either the reference gives only employment verification and the dates of employment, or that all inquiries are sent to HR to respond. This does not help the case of an employee who has a fantastic record of performance, so it seems that some companies may have gone too far.

All states have different laws, and employers need to be aware of these laws. The interviewer has no risk in asking, but the reference could get his company in trouble for not disclosing some types of information.

Be aware also of a false good reference. This takes more skill to detect, but I know of cases where a company did not want to fire an employee, but they made it difficult for the employee, hoping that he would leave. This is true of administrative staff and also higher level employees.

A reference check should be welcomed by that employer because it indicates that the candidate is seriously looking for a new job. A glowing report that is unwarranted could possibly pass the problem on to the new company.

If an employee was terminated and is collecting unemployment, the same incentive for the former employer exists. This is illegal and known as negligent misrepresentation. So if your BS detector goes off or you have a uneasy feeling, either dig deeper or at least document the interaction to look at it in the larger context of the rest of the information you have.

This piece of information may bring clarity to something not fully apparent in the interview, roundtable or Assessment.

I have helped clients write recommendation letters for a "desired departure" that sound good but said nothing of substance. All of the statements are true, but the lack of specificity about job performance should have been a red flag for a future employer.

I recommended the letter because it stands on its own, and if anyone called for a reference, the letter was to be produced, allowing for no follow-up. If you get such a letter, read it carefully and be aware of what is not being said.

The best reference to check may be one that was not provided by the candidate. If someone in your company knows someone in the candidate's current or prior company who is not on the candidate's reference list, try to talk to that person in a casual way to get candid information and opinion.

* * *

Reference checks are an essential piece of the puzzle that is the candidate's job performance.

* * *

For more detail on reference checks, visit PerfectHireBlueprint.com/Resources.

Background Check

The background check is an optional step. We don't always do background checks. Criminal background checks should be required if employees are entering clients' homes, but may not be required if they stay in an office. Driving records should be checked for anyone driving a company vehicle.

We also recommend that a credit check be done for anyone with access to the company's financial accounts. If you want to do a background check, I recommend that you go to National Crime Search (nationalcrimesearch.com). You can go there directly, sign up and get a report with any of this info: criminal history, sex offender status, SSN validation, list of known aliases, list of known addresses, terrorist search, motor vehicle report, credit report, federal district court search, bankruptcy search, federal & state tax lien search, civil litigation search.

Education verification could also be useful. I recently had a client who had "Education: Master's degree preferred" on the job ad for an executive level position. They found out in the first 90 days that the new hire did not have even a Bachelor's degree. The new hire's response was, "it said Master's preferred, but did not say anything about Bachelor's degree." The employee was terminated because the trust was gone, and the employer was partially to blame.

The costs of these checks are surprisingly low in my view for the benefit the information brings. Be sure to follow state and federal law on what is allowed. The background check company will likely be able to help you stay within the law.

Summary & Action Items

The second interview needs to primarily gather more data on the areas of concern from the first interview and the Assessment.

Use the questions provided by the Job Report that pertain to the areas of concern from the Assessment. Based on the answers to the questions, discern if the gaps from the report can be bridged.

Reference Checks

Here are some good questions to ask:

- In what capacity did you work with Joe?
- What were his biggest strengths or value to the group?
- Would you say that Joe was in the top 25% in job performance as compared to his peers?

- If you were managing Joe, what area would you think he could improve most? Is there another?
- In the interview, Joe told me the story about ____. Can you tell me what happened from your perspective?
- Joe seems to be (character trait). Do I have a correct impression of this?

Reference checks are an essential piece of the puzzle that is the candidate's job performance.

- Hiring manager should make the call to get a peer to peer interaction.
- Legal concerns may make it harder to get candid information. The truth and facts are never illegal to convey.
- Listen for what is not said as well as what is said

Background check

Criminal background checks should be required if employees are entering clients' homes or working with sensitive information, but may not be required if they stay in an office. Better safe than sorry, because those you least suspect could be disqualified.

For more information on legal issues and background checks, visit PerfectHireBlueprint.com/Resources.

Chapter 15: Post Interview Roundtable/Interview Candidate Roundtable

The roundtable is a discussion among the people who interviewed the candidate to determine who should be given an offer based on the resume, interviews, Assessments, and reference checks. A roundtable should be run by the hiring manager, or the human resources manager if a better facilitator than the manager.

The assumption is that each interviewer has asked the same questions to each candidate, and each had their own unique questions during the interviews. The goal of the roundtable is to discuss what was asked and what was answered during the interview. This allows everyone to hear the questions and answers.

The hiring manager may have a favorite candidate, so unless the hiring manager can be unbiased, the human resources manager could facilitate the roundtable.

Humans can be manipulative, especially in a situation such as an interview. As stated previously, the gut is difficult to trust by itself with deceptive candidates. This is common, since most are not their natural selves during the interview process. Additional data is needed to confirm or rebut the feelings. Remember that people form an opinion quickly and the interviewer could be using the interview to reinforce the first impression.

A good manager or leader will likely be skilled in influencing, and this can be used to manage the outcome of the roundtable if he or she wants to. I have done it personally. Likewise, in meetings like this roundtable, a more vocal person can sway others who are not strongly in one camp or the other (pro or con). I'll describe how I did it so that you are aware of how it can be done.

Let me first say I did this during a particularly difficult hiring environment where there were more job openings than there were qualified candidates (A-players). I also had an incentivized objective to hire someone that month.

As the hiring manager, I knew I liked a particular candidate (let's call him Joe) after the phone screen. I knew that an interviewer or two may not like Joe as much because I knew what specific interviewers looked for in a candidate (for example, attended a highly ranked school). I knew Joe did not have exactly what they were looking for, but I thought he had great experience and potential.

I quickly debriefed every interviewer as each finished with Joe to gauge if the person was leaning toward yes or no. This was before we met for the roundtable.

I wanted to start the roundtable with a positive note to set the tone, and I wanted to end on a positive note before we voted. Actually, I was the last to speak. A meeting can take on a life of its own when it starts unexpectedly.

While the vote was not binding, and I had the final say, I wanted a super majority before giving an offer to Joe because I wanted to have, ideally, unanimous buy-in. This buy-in is good for morale, and hiring someone without unanimous buy-in has the opposite effect.

There were five people voting, and I had two NOs sandwiched between three YES. I also set a time limit of 5 minutes per person (not just this time, but always) so as not to have a filibuster. The resulting vote was what I had hoped for. Joe would get an offer. (By the way, Joe turned out to be a great fit!)

I do not recommend that any hiring manager should do what I did above. I made my one really bad hiring mistake 20 years ago, when hiring someone I knew socially (unacknowledged bias). I learned my lesson about following the process. It is ideal that you have unanimity with the vote, but you should always have a large majority.

Now to the recommended process:

I recommend at least 3 interviewers (I prefer 5). It is understood that smaller companies will have fewer, and larger companies will typically have more.

As stated in the First Interview chapter, each interviewer should ask different questions from the others, and those questions should align with the person's expertise if possible. The reason to do this is to uncover as much as possible with the most efficient use of time.

If multiple candidates are being interviewed, the same interviewers should ask the same questions in the same way to all candidates to ensure comparing apples to apples.

To make the process "fair," the facilitator (manager or other) should ask each interviewer about their experience with the candidate and how she answered the assigned questions. The order should be lowest rank to highest rank, because the answers of higher ranking people will influence those who rank lower.

The other interviewers should be allowed to ask clarifying questions of the interviewer who is speaking to help them form their own opinions.

While the goal is for everyone to get equal time speaking, there can be a time when a specific candidate answer will spur on more discussion. Suppressing that discussion could hurt full buy-in, but end the discussion when issue is clarified and everyone has been heard.

The decision to do a roundtable on each candidate or to do it on all candidates that have gone through 2 interviews (or one roundtable for Interview 1, another for Interview 2, etc.) depends on the urgency, best candidate timeline and the hiring environment.

If you need someone quickly, have an A-player who needs an answer quickly, or you are in an environment where there are few qualified candidates, then I would recommend that you do a roundtable on each candidate, not waiting for all the interviews to be completed.

This is because the best candidates are in greater demand and could be snapped up by another company before you make an offer. If Einstein applied for a research job, would you wait to interview all of the other candidates before you decided?

To make a hiring decision, the Assessment should make up no more than 1/3rd of the decision. Other components to the hiring decision are the interviews, the job specific test, references, background checks, experience, proximity to work, unexplained job gaps, education level, and responsiveness.

Below is a sample grid that you can use to make a hiring decision. This was adapted from a best practice from a colleague, Simon Young of the Rainmaker Group, who only hires top sales people for companies. Some things are non-negotiable.

You can use this to set expectations and calibrate your interview team. In this model, 100pts is a NO HIRE – the lower the score, the better. You can find this as a spreadsheet for download at PerfectHireBlueprint.com/Resources.

Adapt this to your needs. Build your grid with criteria and point values so that you should not give an offer to anyone over 25 points. If you give an offer to someone who is over 30 points, you are settling. Don't settle - keep looking for a better fit.

Now that the decision has been made to try to get the candidate, it is up to the manager to determine with the help of HR whether they can make an offer that will be accepted.

Non-Negotiable	100 points	10 points	5 points	0 points
Criminal Background	Felony, theft, abuse/ violence	Felony -DUI (use some discretion)	Misdemeanor	No Criminal Record
Education Level	HS Diploma	Some College	4 yr. Degree	Masters in field
References	2 negative	1 Negative, 1 Positive	2 Positive, 1 Negative	3 Positive
Direct experience	None	2 yrs. or less	2 to 5 yrs.	5 yrs.+
Gaps in Work History	Unexplained Gaps	Dubious Gaps	1 Explained Gap	No Gaps
Proximity to Job	Not in area	Willing to commute	Within 40 min of worksite	Lives near worksite
Match to Benchmark (13 matches)	More than one red	Few yellow - maybe 1 red	Blue, green and maybe 1 yellow	All blue, maybe a few green
Interview - Experience questions	Mis-Fit (Poor Answers)	C-Player	B-Player	A-Player (Great Answers)
Interview - Behavioral questions	Mis-Fit (Poor Answers)	C-Player	B-Player	A-Player (Great Answers)
Interview - Motivation questions	Mis-Fit (Poor Answers)	C-Player	B-Player	A-Player (Great Answers)
Interview - Skill Questions	Mis-Fit (Poor Answers)	C-Player	B-Player	A-Player (Great Answers)
Total Points				

Summary & Action Items

The roundtable is a discussion among the people who interviewed the candidate to determine who should be given an offer based on the resume, interviews and Assessments.

- 3-5 interviewers

- Different questions from each interviewer – aligned with expertise

Summary of interview process

- Develop the hiring criteria.
- Ensure each interviewer has unique questions.
- Have each interviewer ask the same questions to all candidates.
- Have a brief roundtable after Interview 1. Send Assessment to all candidates who are going on to interview 2.
- Have a roundtable after interview 2 to determine: hire or no hire.
- Manager/facilitator of roundtable should be objective and fair.
- Have a facilitator of the roundtable if needed.
- Gain unanimity if possible. People need to weigh in to buy in.

Section 3: Closing the Deal

Chapter 16: The Offer

Does it bother you when someone asks a question starting with, "If money were no object, what would you..."? It's hard to make decisions without any concern for what you'd earn or what it would cost.

Recently someone told me that a father with only one daughter said he'd pay any amount for her wedding, but I still think there might have been an upper limit. Even sports teams with rabid fan bases have a salary cap, and some sports markets can pay more than others (luckily for me, my local Boston teams have those fans).

While your company's budget may not be the same as an MLB or NFL team, I'm sure you also have an upper limit. That limit might also be below the current market value for the position that you are hiring.

I think what companies are looking for is the cheapest person who can adequately do the job as they envision it. I think they should be trying to get the person of the most value within the budget. This is the person who may perform at a level much higher than the compensation would normally attract.

First we'll go down the usual path that companies consider regarding compensation, and then we'll discuss something much more strategic when it comes to getting A-players on board.

One client was recently looking for an inside salesperson, and he had a salary range in mind. Although he was not looking for this, he found a candidate with more skills. The candidate could not only be proficient at the inside sales job the day he started, but he also had the short term potential to be an even more valuable outside salesperson.

In this case, the company paid much more than they were budgeting not only to fill the current opening, but also hopefully a future opening.

Another client needed an Accounts Payable specialist initially for a part time position. After 80+ resumes, and many of phone screens and interviews, they offered the job to a woman who had more than enough experience. She was just reentering the workforce after her children reached school age.

The company believes that they got an amazing value, and the employee might be able to transition to full time as the children get older and the company keeps growing.

It is difficult for me to tell you what to offer a candidate because value is in the eye of the beholder. But I can say that you need to think about more than just the cost of hiring – think about the value you will gain.

For instance, a CPA firm might hire someone who works fast and will be billable on her first day. If the firm does fixed-price tax returns, that person is going to bring in a lot of money for the firm.

If the company doesn't feel comfortable about a high price to be paid, consider a variable compensation model. Salespeople are typically paid on commission, and that motivates the type of person who does not want his compensation to be limited and wants to be paid well for performing well. I'm not recommending that everyone be paid on some type of commission, but there are other variable compensation models.

One model that I like and have instituted in many places is the Management by Objective, or MBO. For example, let's take 20% of the person's total compensation and tie it to attaining goals and objectives. Speaking broadly, if the objectives bring in revenue or reduce expenses, then the company may have the money to pay the 20%.

MBOs tend to be performance based, so higher performance pays more, and higher performance can be more profitable, so the personal and company goals are aligned.

There are many details that matter with MBOs, so the right implementation is incredibly important. The thing to remember about paying for results is that you get what you pay for, and there needs to be an awareness of unintended consequences.

One obvious concern is that the person with the variable compensation now becomes keenly aware of what adds money to the paycheck, so "doing the right thing" for the company as a whole may not be in the person's personal financial interest.

The tricky part about compensation is to be aware of what motivates the person. Personal Assessments give an indication of what is important to the individual. If the person is risk averse, then benefits might be more important to them. If the person wants to be seen as successful, then public recognition or a fancy title may be more important than a higher salary.

If the business is small, there is more leeway for compensation variation, and maybe less flexibility on total compensation package. Non-standard compensation becomes unwieldy as the company gets bigger, but consider what motivates the individual to help the company grow when it is small.

* * *

The tricky part about compensation is to be aware of what motivates the person. If the business is small, there is more leeway for compensation variation.

* * *

Small businesses may not be able to compete with larger businesses when it comes to compensation and benefits. But small businesses do offer other intangibles, such as flexibility in work hours that allow people to spend time with children or elderly family. Working from home (or other remote locations like shared office space) is often an added benefit for solo workers.

Small businesses also give employees access to the ultimate decision makers without having to go through the "chain of command" that is required in corporations and other large organizations. They can often offer a larger job scope that provides more variety and a more impressive title. Small businesses have to recognize that these are advantages over larger companies for many people. Uncovering the perks that are important to the prospect is essential in making a successful offer.

It could be that the offer is not for a full time position. Depending on your company policy on benefit eligibility, making the position, say, 32 hours per week could be exactly what the candidate wants. Then you have to determine if that works for the company. Does that mean taking Fridays or Wednesdays off, or does it mean two half days, or maybe 6 ¼ hours a day? Look for the Win/Win agreement that works for both sides.

When an offer is given, the hiring manger should have a good idea that it will be accepted. The salary requirements and other NEEDS should have been uncovered and explored before the offer is given.

Other needs could include:

- Insurance and other benefits
- Vacation already scheduled
- A week of unpaid vacation because 2 weeks off just isn't enough
- Upcoming Paternity leave
- Times when the candidate cannot work
- Work/life balance – whatever that is for the candidate
  - Family time

- o   Time for themselves
- o   Time to volunteer
- Any relocation expenses that the candidate cannot absorb to take the job
- Other short-term transition-related expenses or concerns.

Now let's consider a more strategic and less traditional way to determine what the applicant needs to decide to come to your company, and stay long term.

Ask yourself, "Why would an A-player come to your company?" For most it is not the compensation – it is whether the work is motivating or not. What motivates each candidate will be different, and you need to know that the position and compensation will motivate her before you make an offer.

The vast majority (>80%) of people change jobs for a significant career move, while a much smaller number (<20%) make lateral moves. A significant career move does not necessarily mean "for money."

There are three things that will get people to move other than money:
1. Does the job stretch their abilities?
2. Will job satisfaction be higher?
3. Will there be more job growth than the current job?

If the person can easily answer yes to two or more of these, then compensation will not be an issue as long as it is fair.

How do you know if the offer will be accepted?

If the interviews were conducted properly, the candidate should be champing at the bit to get an offer and accept it. If the job is a great fit, there is a positive career move, the conversations with the interviewers were positive, the company is a great fit, you have built a good rapport as the hiring manager, and the compensation is on par or better, you should be able to close the candidate.

If you don't know for certain that your offer will be accepted, then you have missed some steps in the earlier stages.

Some people will tell you that they have a feeling that the offer will be accepted, but how do you know (back to the discussion on trusting your gut)? I recommend that you ASK.

This was discussed at the end of the second interview. This is the second part of the trial lawyer analogy. I mentioned that trial lawyers shouldn't ask questions of witnesses on the stand where the answer isn't already known. If there is a surprise at this point, something has changed. In the TV or Movie drama, the opposing party typically made threats that changed the story of the witness.

In making an offer, it is usually nothing quite so nefarious. In most cases something has happened in the candidate's personal life, or another job offer has been presented. Keep tabs on your top candidates throughout the process.

After the roundtable you should know who your first choice is. I would approach that candidate and tell her that it is looking like you are going to give her an offer, but you still need to gather more data (the reference checking and any other background checks and tests that you require).

At that time, I would say, "If we did offer you a job, would you accept it?" I know that she has no concrete data on the offer, but she should know all about the benefits by now, and she may have done her homework enough to know what a typical employee in that same position would make.

In Massachusetts starting in 2018, you can't ask about the candidate's current salary. The "Equal Pay Law" makes that illegal. You can only ask for the person's salary requirements. Other states may follow, so check your local laws.

In the movie The Firm, Tom Cruise's character, Mitch McDeere, had to figure out what his offer was without opening the envelope. He had to ask questions to figure it out, but they never told him and he brought the envelope home, unopened, knowing what is contained.

Your candidate can know what you might offer before you offer it. If she does not say immediately that she would take it, ask her what she'd want the offer letter to say. Or, you could take the approach of "on a scale of 1-10, how likely are you to take our offer?" If the number is not 8 or above, keep digging.

It might not be about the pay. No amount of money will be able to compensate for a job that does not motivate an applicant. I know that this isn't always easy to bring up (or get a straight answer) because it is not what the candidate expects.

Once you give the offer in writing, you've lost control of the negotiation. If you don't get this right, the negotiation may just be starting.

In big companies, an offer packet needs to be created for signoff at upper levels. It needs to include the total compensation with benefits, relocation and signing bonus, if applicable. It needs the resume, cover letter, and anything that came out during the interview. It needs an Equal Employment Opportunity (EEO) form, and the Assessment if one is given. The reference checks and another other testing results need to be in the packet. Then it needs to get signatures from HR, Finance and at least one or two managers.

Why would you want to go through all of that if you didn't know that the offer would be accepted? What if the candidate is just trying to get a raise at his current job, or looking to negotiate a higher price on another job offer? Unless you can make an offer like the one The Firm gave to Mitch (Mercedes-Benz, low interest mortgage and 10% above any other offer), you don't know that the candidate will accept it.

If you are worried about offering too much and throwing off your compensation structure, consider a "signing bonus." This is a one-time deal sweetener that won't come back to haunt you every year. Even in times when the hiring market was not very competitive, I typically gave a small signing bonus because it was unexpected, was very meaningful to the candidate, and helped ensure a motivated new hire.

If you finally get all of the information you need and propose a win/win acceptable offer, you won't have to worry about the candidate waiting for another offer or surprisingly not showing up on day 1. Then again, you always have to worry about the latter – more on that in the next chapter.

Vocalizing the offer always seems to be a bit awkward. You hope the candidate is excited about the offer, and she is hoping that the offer is good. I always liked to give the offer face-to-face to see the person's reaction.

You should discuss how the company is doing and how future coworkers are looking forward to having the position filled, etc. If you are getting nods as you speak, the candidate might be ready for the offer. To transition into that discussion, use language like, "We've interviewed [X number of] candidates and some were very good. The hiring team agrees with me that we should offer you the job. We think you will fit in well, add to our culture and have the opportunity to grow professionally. So I've got an offer here that I think you will be happy with."

Ask if she can accept the offer on the spot. If it is accepted, GREAT! You've done a great job to get a candidate that fits.

Whether it is accepted or not, you still need to take the steps in the next chapter.

Summary & Action Items

When an offer is given, the hiring manger should have a good idea that it will be accepted. The salary requirements and other NEEDS should have been uncovered and explored before the offer is given.

Other needs could include:

- Insurance and other benefits
- Vacation already scheduled
- Upcoming familial leave
- Times when the candidate cannot work
- Work/life balance – whatever that is for the candidate
- Family time
- Time for themselves
- Time to volunteer
- Any relocation expenses that the candidate will absorb to take the job

Chapter 17: Post Offer

Congratulations, you've followed an effective process to get the right candidates into interviews, interviewed well, checked all the data you can find on the candidate, made an offer, and it was accepted. You should feel good about yourself - you are done, right? **Wrong.** You are not done until the candidate shows up for work and gets through Day 1.

We've seen situations where a candidate will verbally accept a job offer, then change her mind the next day. You then have to re-open the job listing, start sourcing candidates and start the whole process over again. The steps below will outline how to prevent this. It may appear to be over the top, but I can tell you that it works!

We've been in a market that is candidate friendly for a while, and if you make an offer to the perfect candidate, you need to ensure that she will show up. Here's how to make sure she comes aboard (substitute parent/significant other for spouse if appropriate):

1. **Make an offer** that the candidate will happily accept. Make sure the position provides an opportunity for professional development. It may also include an unexpected bonus just to get the candidate excited about the job. Tell her that you fought for more incentives, as another way to motivate her.

2. **Make it stick** – Ask her, "Is this decision yours alone? Does anyone else have a say in this decision?" Even if she says no, ask, "What will your spouse think of this decision? Will your spouse be fully supportive?" If there is hesitation, you don't have a deal yet.

3. If #2 is not a solid answer, **walk the candidate through** this process. The following may sound too direct,

so make it less confrontational and just part of the conversation:

  a. "What will your spouse say?"

  b. "Why are you accepting this offer? Is it a better opportunity than your current job? Be ready to tell your spouse why this job is a better fit. Do you think the reasons are convincing? Why is this transition good for your spouse?"

  c. Is there anyone else who will influence this decision? Walk through b. again for this person.

4. **Leaving is hard** – "When you give your notice for your current position, what reaction do you expect?"

  a. "Will they be happy for you?"

  b. "Will they want you to stay more than 2 weeks?"

  c. "Will they be unhappy and walk you to the door?"

  d. "Will they counter-offer with, 'What will it take for you to stay?'" (This question will expose whether you are being used to get a raise at the current position.)

      i. "If they do, what will you do?"

      ii. "If you decide to stay,

          1. do you think your wanting to leave will shake the trust they have in you? If so, do you think that may put a target on your back?"

          2. "Will the reasons that you want to leave now change? Will you want to

leave only a few months from now when nothing really changes?"

 iii. I recommend that you go in and tell them, "I'm giving my notice today. I've given this a lot of thought, and this is an opportunity that is great for me. I've fully considered this and my mind is made up."

 iv. If they push further, tell them, "There is nothing you can say that will convince me to stay. I am excited for the transition and so is my family. Please don't try to jump through hoops to keep me. It may be flattering to me, but the basic reasons for leaving will not change."

  1. The candidate is saving them all the work that it would take to counter offer.

PHB Tip: By the way, if the old company counter offers, the candidate will look to you to sweeten the deal. Nip that in the bud. That is why you tell them up front that you fought for them and gave them a very good, motivating offer. She is less likely to come back asking for more if she feels you've already fought for her.

  2. If she rejected the counter offer, more bad feelings would result. Terms like ungrateful and manipulative may be used.

5. **Test the eagerness of the candidate** – "Would you like some pre-work that you can do before you arrive to ensure you hit the ground running?"

 a. If she answers yes, you should feel pretty good that she will show up.

b. If she answers no, pause and let her fill in the dead air. She'll either reconsider or answer why she will not have time to look at it before she starts.

c. Either way, this question can give you more certainty depending on the answer.

6. **To really seal the deal**, send flowers (or something the spouse might like) to the house with a note, "Welcome to our family. We'll be even better with you on the team."

a. If there was any doubt in her mind, her guilt and/or her spouse's will prevent any reconsideration.

b. This gives the spouse confidence that the new company cares and that the right choice was made.

c. An alternative (or supplement) would be to send some company clothing that can help them envision being part of the team.

And you thought you were done when you gave an offer!

Follow this process, and your perfect hire will show up eager to contribute immediately.

<u>**Summary & Action Items**</u>

Make an offer that the candidate will happily accept.

Now ask – "Is this decision yours alone? Does anyone else have a say in this decision?"

If #2 is not a solid answer, walk the candidate through the process outlined in this chapter.

Offer to First Day flowchart:

Give the offer

   Was it accepted immediately?

      YES – Make it stick and coach

      NO – How will the decision be made?

   Are you happy with the decision process?

      YES – Coach and give tips

      NO – Walk through the steps, role play and coach

   How and when will you give your notice?

   (Confident in answer?)

      YES – Get commitment and seal the deal

      NO – How and when will you give your notice?

Chapter 18: Onboarding

Now that you've hired the best value candidate and an A-player, how do you keep her excited about the opportunity? She has made the decision to leave where she was to join your company, and likely is expecting this change to be a great career move.

But if the new company throws the new employee right into the job without any training, or worse gives her little direction, she's less likely to be a successful long-term employee:

- the excitement will dissipate
- resentment may creep in
- fear of doing the wrong things
- career path uncertainty
- wonder how promotions are made
- company/personal mission mismatch
- lack of HR compliance
- lack of connection with other employees

60% of companies don't set onboarding goals. This often leads to dissent among new employees, hence, companies lose 25% of all new employees in the first year. This is not only frustrating, but also expensive, since the average cost to fill a position was $11,000 without relocation (2012 Allied Workforce Mobility Survey - Gallup).

I hate to see this happen at companies – that's why there should be an emphasis on onboarding. This PHB process can also generate a "development plan" that is based on what the Benchmark indicates is desirable. This can be a good guide for the first 90 days.

Onboarding is a big topic, but this is a book on hiring. To get the full overview on how to do onboarding correctly, go to the website PerfectHireBlueprint.com/Onboarding and get the eBook that covers the topic fully.

You have invested a great number of resources to get the candidate this far. Finish the job to help ensure the perfect new hire will stick.

Chapter 19: Benefits of This Process

When the Perfect Hire Blueprint process is followed, the likelihood of a great hire is very high. If shortcuts are taken, this increases the possibility of a Mis-fit. Other benefits include:

- Perception that the company is ethical, selective (full of A-players), and thoughtful.
    - Ethical – follows the rules and laws
    - Selective – enables the cream to rise to the top
    - Thoughtful – treats candidates with respect
- Confidence that laws are not broken
- Better retention – existing employees recognize the benefits of the process, and they appreciate the quality of new hires
- Efficiency – spend time only with the right people and doing the right things in the business
- Saving money – cuts the cost of a Mis-fit
- Reduces bias in hiring, enabling more diversity
- Increasing customer satisfaction – clients only deal with A-players
- May increase margins – customers will pay more for a better service or product, and fewer mistakes leads to fewer product returns
- Lower overhead – A-players need less supervision: should be able to reduce the manager to employee ratio
- Life balance – leaders worry less because they trust the competence of the team, and the leaders are called less after hours to clean up mistakes
- More time on strategy – if managers are not dealing with problem employees, they can focus on growth

Objections

Objection: Hiring A-Players is TOO EXPENSIVE.

While it may be true that A-players earn more than B-players, the increased revenue and lower number of issues will recoup that salary difference multiple times over. According to an Oracle study in 2012, "... high performers in operations roles are able to increase productivity by 40 percent, high performers in management roles increase profits by 49 percent, and in sales positions high performers are responsible for 67 percent greater revenue."

Objection: Our experience is that hiring is just a shot in the dark. That is why we have a probation period.

What A-player in her right mind would leave her old job where she has a great reputation to jump to a new job where she starts on probation? The probation program virtually guarantees that you will not get A-players. People willing to be on probations are either escaping their current job or are unemployed. Either of these are typically not a good source of A-players (though we acknowledge that all situations are unique).

Objection: Headhunters/recruiters charge too much.

When there is an abundance of good talent available, we agree! In times of low unemployment and economic expansion, the A-players are just not looking for jobs. In these times, good recruiters will entice A-players to look at new opportunities. If your company can't grow or is losing money because you can't find the right people, recruiters may be the only option, but we would recommend trying the non-recruiting options first if filling the position is not urgent. Use the PHB process.

Objection: Assessments are not accurate.

We agree that there are Assessments that are not very accurate. Some may not have enough research or science behind them to prove validity. Some are intended for a different purpose and are being used for hiring. We use the TTI TriMetrix HD Assessment which includes behaviors, motivators, soft skills and acumen.

These are backed by decades of research and more recently validated with brain science. Brain scans have been used to verify that the Assessments are triggering the correct part of the brain, including checking languages other than English. With this we know that candidates need to take the Assessment in their native language for the highest accuracy.

Chapter 20: Why I Use TTI Assessments

There are a lot of Assessments available today. The Assessments that I use are the best for me and my clients. I've taken all kinds of Assessments in the past. The first one that I remember taking was Myers-Briggs (now MBTI) years ago, and it was insightful. I was later introduced to DISC, which has a similar lineage, and I found it better for me and I'll tell you why below. There are many companies that offer DISC, just as many offer MBTI, but they are not all equal.

Other Assessments do exist. Some are still being used because "that is what we've always used," and some are trendy for a while (like StrengthsFinder). The marketing for many is good, and some have strong sales teams. I can't say that I've taken them all, but I've taken many, and I have chosen the Assessments from TTI Success Insights because they have everything that I think is needed, including Benchmarking. They are unbiased, normed internationally, and validated. TTI Assessments are consistently referred to as "best in class" in side-by-side comparisons with competitors in immediate impact and completeness.

Company	Behaviors	Motivators	Hartman/ Acumen	Competencies	EQ	Sales Skills	360 Survey	Job Match Comparison	Adverse Impact	Validation for Selection	International Norming
TTI SI	X	X	X	X	X	X	X	X	X	X	X

I have met the founder and know the leaders of the company. I attend their annual conference and keep my certifications current. They are in the business for all the right reasons, and while I think their Assessments are the best today, they are not sitting on their laurels; the Assessments are improving every year. Here are some of the key items to look for in Assessments:

Accurate/Predictive

My clients and I have found the results to not only give us insight into the person being assessed, but they also give us a view into the future. TTI just reaffirmed the validity of Behaviors and Motivators via an independent study in 2015.

To ensure the accuracy of the Assessment, it can be taken in the native language of the candidate. This is because it is difficult to fully grasp the English language with what I call "loaded words." As an example, the word "Welfare" has a negative connotation to many conservative people in the US. Canada is much more liberal, having an extensive welfare system that includes free health and medical care, and it is ranked as one of the top 5 countries to live in by the UN. TTI uses neuroscience to ensure that the words used trigger the desired parts of the brain, and that is best done through one's native language.

Understandable

Unlike other Assessments, the TTI Assessments make sense to the typical reader who has not spent hours trying to understand the jargon. For example, if your spouse were to read your completed Assessment, the result is (more often than not) laughter and exclamations of "that's so true." This reaction is common not only because the Assessment is accurate, but also because the reader understands it. Even though the Assessment is based in science, the report does not read like a research paper.

The laughter comes from pointing out all the traits and habits that have been observed. This is not new; Jerry Seinfeld (and Larry David) made a living of pointing out the obvious to get laughs. The humor was not highbrow, it was pointing out the funny in everyday life.

The terminology is not the use of 4 letters, but uses clear language such as Conductor, Persuader or Analyzer. The average person can visualize someone when they hear the term. These terms are accessible to all employees and can be used in work interactions. INTJ is just not as useful for most people.

I recommend that co-workers who may not know each other well should let the other read their Assessment. This gives both the insight into the other that can forge strong relationships and very high productivity. When there is conflict, I don't recommend just letting the other read the report. Use an intermediary along with the reports because there is a higher chance of manipulation, since there isn't good will from the beginning.

Applicable

The information in the Assessments can be applied immediately. The information can shape a new hire's onboarding plan, or an employee's performance plan, or for setting goals. The reports give the reader ways to successfully interact with the person assessed. This leads to fewer misunderstandings and ultimately helps create a work environment for all employees to thrive.

A manager should review the Assessment results periodically to be reminded of strengths, weaknesses, and preferences. This can enable a strong direct relationship and team dynamic.

Safe for Hiring

I see the interviewer's biases all the time when hiring. Sometimes it is subtle, but other times it is overt. I've had hiring managers say that they prefer only men or only women, and only in a certain age range, or only married. We discuss this when creating a job Benchmark, but none of this appears in the Benchmark Assessment. And I have seen that when a Benchmark is used, biases are reconsidered.

While the interviewers may have a bias, the Assessments need to not disfavor or exclude members of a protected category disproportionally. TTI completed an Adverse Impact Study in 2014 that concluded that there is no evidence that the Assessments could cause adverse impact with regard to gender, race, disability or veteran status. Their products are Safe Harbor-approved, non-discriminatory and are fully compliant with hiring laws and regulations including EEOC and OFCCP. Everyone has biases, and it is comforting to know that the Assessments can contribute to objectivity.

Note: At the time of this printing, the Emotional Quotient report is not yet approved for hiring. I use it extensively for employee development, especially in managers, leaders and anyone with significant customer contact. Unlike the other Assessments where there is no right answer, it is generally accepted that higher EQ scores are better than lower. There will likely be more research on this, but my initial view is that women tend to have higher EQ scores than men on average, and older people have higher EQ scores than younger people on average. Unless there is proof that there is not built in bias, these Assessments should not be used in hiring decisions.

Continuous Education

TTI continually educates and recertifies their certified Value Added Associates (VAA). To ensure the person getting the report understands the results, the Assessments are not sold by TTI to the company that is hiring. The Assessment is administered by a VAA and the report is debriefed with the end client so that the report is fully understood in the context of the intended job. The reports are easily digestible, but there are important nuances and report interactions that only a Certified VAA who has debriefed many Assessments can fully understand. I have delivered hundreds (approximately 1000) of reports, and each time the reports are improved, there is even more data that can be gleaned from the combination of Assessments. Research PHDs are on staff that refine the Assessments and train the VAAs on the proper use of the information.

Social Proof

Over 100,000 companies have used TTI Assessments. Over 22 Million TTI SI Assessments have been taken since 2000, and another Assessment is taken every 7 seconds around the world. TTI is written up in business journals and often quoted as being an authority on unbiased, accurate Assessments.

Science of Self

TTI does extensive research to ensure the Assessments trigger the appropriate parts of the brain. They also confirm that the score matches the brain activity that should give that result. This is also used in validating the Assessment accuracy in other languages. I know of no other Assessment company that puts this level of research into their products. This allows TTI Assessments to not only be accurate, but to be advancing on a continual basis.

For over 30 years, TTI has researched and applied social and brain science, creating behavioral Assessments that consultants all over the world use to hire, develop and retain the best talent in the world.

Rank Order	TriMetrix® DNA Soft Skill	AAD	Gamma Image
1	Presenting	-0.91	
2	Diplomacy	-0.89	
3	Customer Service	-0.86	
4	Self-Management	-0.40	
5	Interpersonal Skills	-0.37	
6	Employee Development/ Coaching	0.21	

Brain scan of person taking Competencies/Soft Skills Assessment

You can see more at ttisuccessinsights.com/research

For these reasons and many more, TTI is my "go to" company, and the TriMetrix HD Assessment is what I count on for hiring A-players. To see samples of the reports mentioned in this process, visit PerfectHireBlueprint.com/Resources.

For more information about TTI, visit ttisuccessinsights.com/why-tti.

If you'd like to see what the report says about you, fill out the form at PerfectHireBlueprint.com/Resources. I have a limited number of copies for readers of this book (unless you bought a bundle with the book containing an Assessment), so don't wait to inquire.

TTI Assessments are only available from certified Value Added Associates. You will see how accurate the Assessments are after you take one. If you are as impressed as I think you will be, I can set up an account for you where you can administer the reports for your company.

Just fill out the form at PerfectHireBlueprint.com/Resources and I will recommend the right Assessment(s) for your needs.

Chapter 21: Takeaways

Hiring the right people can make or break a business. Every hire is important when a company is small; some of these hires will be your future leaders, and key positions of leadership are critically important in growing companies.

All customer facing positions are important because they are the window to the customer base. The quality of the people and the fit within the company culture determines if the person will thrive in the position.

The sum of the hires determines the growth trajectory of the company. A-players, while they may cost a little more, are worth it since you'll get a higher multiple of ROI on A-players than B-players or lower.

Don't settle; work hard and recruit the right person who is the perfect hire for the job and the company. Start the ball rolling by hiring one A-player – then that one will attract another, and another. Soon you can focus on your business rather than your employee issues.

Follow the Perfect Hire Blueprint to stop making the hiring mistakes that plague companies of all sizes. Every step is critical, so don't skip any. Lack of execution on any step, even if every other step went well, could allow a Mis-fit into your company.

Adding EEOC and OFCCP compliant Assessments will uncover blind spots and biases to take your hiring process to the next level – one that attracts A-players and leads to the retention of existing employees.

For additional resources visit PerfectHireBlueprint.com. There you will find more detailed information about hiring and retaining

A-players, samples of the Assessments that I use, and an opportunity to take the Assessment yourself to see how "spot-on" it is in capturing the whole person. Take the guesswork out of hiring!

Now that you know the secret to consistent company growth, why would you risk your company by ignoring this advice and continuing to hire with your gut? It's your company – I want you to beat the odds, and grow a successful and profitable business.

To your success!

* * *

What Are People Saying?

"Dave Clough has written a must-read for any person who is hiring talent for his or her company. He carefully walks you through a practical guide to discovering and engaging the best talent in any industry. Read this book and learn from one of the best."

- Rick Bowers, President of Global Distribution, TTI Success Insights

"David Clough and his crew were invaluable in my efforts to hire an Administrative Assistant in my accounting practice. His company placed the online ads and did the initial screening which eliminated all people who did not have the skills to perform the work or were located hundreds (or thousands) of miles away. They also did the next screening to look more deeply into their background and do the initial telephone interview.

They presented us with a list of candidates and we then took over and did the in person interviews. The candidates took the TriMetrix Assessment and Dave went over the results of the test with me and made his recommendations.

The results have been spectacular. The person we hired has been much better than we had anticipated when we first started the process. She has been with us for three tax seasons now and is constantly looking to improve what she does and to take on more responsibility.

I highly recommend Dave & his company if you are trying to add good people to your team."

- Thomas Arrison, Vallas & Arrison, PC

**From the company that hired a senior engineer
referenced on Page 7:**

"So far so good. He seems to be catching on quickly. He's
enthusiastic and tells us he really enjoys what he's doing. I believe
he's going to work out fine!"

- Steven Powers, President, Intrepid Advisors LLC

"Dave was hired to consult our Club on the hiring process. A big
part of our success was from implementing the Assessment within
our hiring process. The Benchmarking part was incredibly helpful.
Comparing a candidate's attributes to our ideal employee was
invaluable and gave us the confidence to make hard decisions on
potential hires. Over the past 4 years with Dave's systems, I have
hired over 10 employees and each one has been an asset to our
company. I would recommend Dave to any company looking to
improve their hiring process as well as improving or creating the
right culture."

- Jason Deranian, Director of Fitness & Sales, Mount Auburn
Athletic Club

"As a hiring manager of a small organization, it's stressful and
time consuming find that "right" candidate that meets all your
criteria of skill, innate talent, and personality that fits the position
and company culture. All are important in order to keep talented
people invested and engaged with the hopes of keeping your
employee with the organization for years instead of months.

Leaving the hiring process to an outsider seemed risky. There was
also no time to waste. My fears were put to rest when I contracted
Dave Clough to work on a hire with me two years ago. Dave
delivers on describing his process and delivering on that process
on time. The unique Assessment he uses and analysis in the

process is dead on accurate. Not only does the Assessment report bring the right candidates to the forefront, but this information is incredibly useful in training and managing your new employee. I found the information so incredibly helpful and the ramp up and managing was much smoother due to the detailed Assessment results regarding core strengths and communication styles of the new employee.

Consulting with Dave is one of the best investments I have made to date in our organization. Good people are important to companies and their success and I would not have been able to find the best possible talent for our organization without his help."

- Trudy Khosla, Acton Congregational Church

* * *

If you're interested in more information, visit perfecthireblueprint.com.

About the Author

Dave Clough is the owner and principal of Clough and Associates, DBA mPower Advisors. He works with small business owners to help enable them to succeed and grow their businesses by getting the right people in the company, making sure those people have the tools needed to thrive, and putting the right systems in place.

In addition to his consulting practice started in 2004, Dave was also the COO for a few startups. Dave's large company experience came primarily from 13 years of holding multiple field management positions at Synopsys, Inc., an Electronic Design software company. He started his career as an electrical engineer and project manager at Raytheon Company, designing satellite communications equipment.

He was certified as an Executive Associate by the Institute for Independent Business in 2004 and as an Accredited Mentor by CMT International in 2006. Dave is also a Certified Professional Analyst for Behaviors, Motivators, DNA Emotional Quotient, TriMetrix HD, and Stages of Growth by TTI Success Insights. Dave has helped over 100 companies of all types from 1 to over 150 employees enhance their businesses.

Dave has deep expertise in business coaching, strategy, employee and leadership development, inter-generational working environment (Millennials to Boomers), recruiting and hiring A-players, retaining the best employees, sales management and training, marketing, owner productivity, customer support, professional services, motivation, and many more.

Dave is nominally on multiple boards and is a speaker at conferences on many of the topics mentioned above.

Dave was born and raised in the blue collar town of Claremont, NH. He came from a poor background and dramatically improved his station in life, the way most people would expect. It was a bit of a fluke for him to take this path, considering that he was a middle child of a fractured family of 8 that was on food stamps and free lunch when Dave was in middle school. Going to college was not only unexpected, but also challenging in so many ways, including self-funding as an independent student.

Dave's path

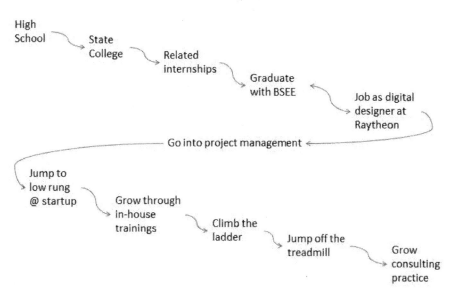

Simon Sinek's book *Start with Why* outlines how finding your passion will help you find success professionally and personally, and drive others to succeed as well.

Dave's "why," and his passion, is to help small businesses (1 to 350 employees) succeed. He left corporate America in 2004 to do just that, start his own business advisory company. The reason he cares so much about small businesses is because they are an economic equalizer and a way to change your station in life. Just earning a paycheck may not dramatically change your station in life, but owning a business very well could, and a college education is not a requirement for success.

Many of the small business CEOs/owners Dave has coached have not gone the college route, and his upbringing allows him to better connect with them. Dave's stepfather, who entered the army rather than attending college, bought a small business when Dave was young, but it did not succeed. All of these factors have played a part in forming Dave's "why."

Dave has been able to achieve a life that he did not foresee as a teen. His journey led him from NH, to MA and extensive travel. Dave recently moved back to NH, where he continues his work in a location with many wonderful recreational distractions.

60407013R00117

Made in the USA
Middletown, DE
29 December 2017